CW00601146

for GCSE

Exclusively endorsed and approved by AQA

Series Editor
Paul Metcalf

Series Advisor
David Hodgson

Lead Author
Margaret Thornton

June Haighton
Anne Haworth
Janice Johns
Steven Lomax
Andrew Manning
Kathryn Scott
Chris Sherrington
Mark Willis

FOUNDATION
Module 3

Nelson Thornes
a-Wolters Kluwer business

Published in 2006 by:
Nelson Thornes Ltd
Delta Place
27 Bath Road
CHELTENHAM
GL53 7TH
United Kingdom

06 07 08 09 10 / 10 9 8 7 6 5 4 3

A catalogue record for this book is available from the British Library.

ISBN 0 7487 9756 4

Cover photograph: Swan by Mark Hamblin/OSF/Photolibrary
Illustrations by Roger Penwill
Page make-up by MCS Publishing Services Ltd, Salisbury, Wiltshire

Printed in Great Britain by Scotprint

Acknowledgements

The authors and publishers wish to thank the following for their contribution:
David Bowles for providing the Assess questions
David Hodgson for reviewing draft manuscripts

Thank you to the following schools:
Little Heath School, Reading
The Kingswinford School, Dudley
Thorne Grammar School, Doncaster

The publishers thank the following for permission to reproduce copyright material:

Explore photos
Diver – Corel 55 (NT); Astronaut – Digital Vision 6 (NT);
Mountain climber – Digital Vision XA (NT); Desert explorer – Martin Harvey/Alamy.

British banknotes – Corel 590 (NT); Lighthouse – Corel 502 (NT);
Rows of Colorful Seats in Empty Stadium – Paul Gun/CORBIS;
US Dollar bill – Photodisc 68 (NT); Coins – Corel 633 (NT);
Students in exam – Digital Stock 10 (NT); Discs – Nick Koudis/Photodisc 37 (NT);
Goldfish – Alex Homer; Duke on the Crater's Edge – NASA, John W. Young;
An Ancient Storm in the Jovian Atmosphere – NASA, The Hubble Heritage Team, STScI, AURA, Amy Simon Cornell.

The publishers have made every effort to contact copyright holders but apologise if any have been overlooked.

Contents

Introduction

This book has been written by teachers and examiners who not only want you to get the best grade you can in your GCSE exam but also to enjoy maths.

Each chapter has the following stages:

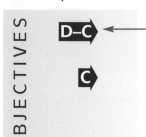

OBJECTIVES

The objectives at the start of the chapter give you an idea of what you need to do to get each grade. Remember that the examiners expect you to perform well at the lower grade questions on the exam paper in order to get the higher grades. So, even if you are aiming for a C grade you will still need to do well on the G grade questions on the exam paper.

Key information and examples to show you how to do each topic. There are several Learn sections in each chapter.

Questions that allow you to practise what you have just learned.

Means that these questions should be attempted with a calculator.

Means that these questions are practice for the non-calculator paper in the exam and should be attempted without a calculator.

Get Real! *These questions show how the maths in this topic can be used to solve real-life problems.*

1 *Underlined questions are harder questions.*

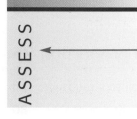

Open-ended questions to extend what you have just learned. These are good practice for your coursework task.

ASSESS

End of chapter questions written by an examiner.

Some chapters feature additional questions taken from real past papers to further your understanding.

1 Integers

OBJECTIVES

G **Examiners would normally expect students who get a G grade to be able to:**

Understand positive and negative integers

Find the factors of a number

F **Examiners would normally expect students who get an F grade also to be able to:**

Add and subtract negative integers

E **Examiners would normally expect students who get an E grade also to be able to:**

Multiply and divide negative integers

C **Examiners would normally expect students who get a C grade also to be able to:**

Recognise prime numbers

Find the reciprocal of a number

Find the least common multiple (LCM) of two simple numbers

Find the highest common factor (HCF) of two simple numbers

Write a number as a product of prime factors

What you should already know ...

- Understand the four rules of number
- Understand place value
- Understand the inequality signs $<$, $>$, $\leqslant$ and $\geqslant$
- Know the meaning of 'sum' and 'product'
- Change a decimal into a fraction
- Change a mixed number into a top-heavy fraction

VOCABULARY

Counting number or **natural number** – a positive whole number, for example, 1, 2, 3, ...

Positive number – a number greater than 0; it can be written with or without a positive sign, for example, 1, $+4$, 8, 9, $+10$, ...

Negative number – a number less than 0; it is written with a negative sign, for example, -1, -3, -7, -11, ...

Integer – any positive or negative whole number or zero, for example, -2, -1, 0, 1, 2, ...

Directed number – a number with a positive or negative sign attached to it; it is often seen as a temperature, for example, -1, $+1$, $+5$, $-3°C$, $+2°C$, ...

Less than ($<$) – the number on the left-hand side of the sign is smaller than that on the right-hand side

Greater than (>) – the number on the left-hand side of the sign is larger than that on the right-hand side

Sum – to find the sum of two numbers, you add them together

Product – the result of multiplying together two (or more) numbers, variables, terms or expressions

Factor – a natural number which divides exactly into another number (no remainder); for example, the factors of 12 are 1, 2, 3, 4, 6, 12

Multiple – the multiples of a number are the products of the multiplication tables, for example, the multiples of 3 are 3, 6, 9, 12, 15, ...

Least common multiple (LCM) – the least multiple which is common to two or more numbers, for example,

the multiples of 3 are 3, 6, 9, 12, 15, 18, 24, 27, 30, 33, 36, ...
the multiples of 4 are 4, 8, 12, 16, 20, 24, 28, 32, 36, ...
the common multiples are 12, 24, 36, ...
the least common multiple is 12

Common factor – factors that are in common for two or more numbers, for example,

the factors of 6 are 1, 2, 3, 6
the factors of 9 are 1, 3, 9
the common factors are 1 and 3

Highest common factor (HCF) – the highest factor that two or more numbers have in common, for example,

the factors of 16 are 1, 2, 4, 8, 16
the factors of 24 are 1, 2, 3, 4, 6, 8, 12, 24
the common factors are 1, 2, 4, 8
the highest common factor is 8

Prime number – a natural number with exactly two factors, for example, 2 (factors are 1 and 2), 3 (factors are 1 and 3), 5 (factors are 1 and 5), 7, 11, 13, 17, 23, ..., 59, ...

Index notation – when a product such as $2 \times 2 \times 2 \times 2$ is written as 2^4, the number 4 is the index (plural **indices**)

Reciprocal – any number multiplied by its reciprocal equals one; one divided by a number will give its reciprocal, for example,

the reciprocal of 3 is $\frac{1}{3}$ because $3 \times \frac{1}{3} = 1$

Learn 1   Positive and negative integers

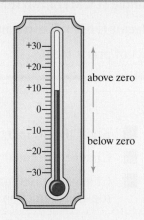

above zero

below zero

Directed numbers are used to show temperatures above and below zero

Example: Put these numbers in ascending order.
+3, −8, −12, +20, −24, −2

In ascending order the numbers are
−24, −12, −8, −2, +3, +20

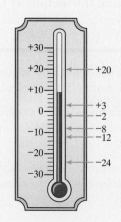

Apply 1

1 Put these numbers in ascending order:

    a +3, 0, − 7, + 6, + 1, + 10, − 5, − 1, + 9

    b − 4, − 9, + 8, 9, 12, + 6, − 7, − 3, 0

    c 67, − 9, + 78, − 98, 876, − 987, 634

2 Write down a number that is less than each of these.

    a −4   **b** −3   **c** −6   **d** −7

3 A thermometer shows 5 degrees below freezing. Write this as a directed number.

4 Get Real!

Clare is £162 overdrawn at the bank. Write this as a directed number.

5 Get Real!

In Plymouth the temperature was − 1°C. In Manchester on the same night, the temperature was − 4°C. Which city was warmer and by how much?

6 Put the correct sign, <, > or =, between these numbers.

    a − 4 ☐ − 9   **b** − 3 ☐ − 2   **c** − 6 ☐ 4   **d** 5 ☐ − 5   **e** 6 ☐ + 6

7 Alison is going sailing.
    She starts from her home which is 300 m above sea level. She walks to the marina where she gets her boat.
    After setting sail she decides to drop anchor and swim. She dives in and goes 5 m under water.
    She sees a turtle swimming.
    What is the height difference between her house and the turtle?

8 Make up your own story to include positive and negative numbers.
    Draw a diagram to show the information.

9 Find the largest four-figure number that can be made using each of the numbers once.

    a 3 4 8 2   **b** 1 5 9 6   **c** 2 6 7 8

10 Find the smallest four-figure number that can be made using each of the numbers once.

    a 3 4 8 2   **b** 1 5 9 6   **c** 2 6 7 8

11 Find all the four-figure numbers that can be made using each of the digits once.
    Arrange them in ascending order.

    a 4 5 2 1   **b** 3 8 6 4   **c** 1 7 9 2

12 Get Real!

You want as much money as possible in your bank account. Put these amounts in order of preference.

a £140, £20 (overdrawn), £150 (credit), £200 (overdrawn), £30 (credit)

b £200, −£150, £30 (credit), −£125, £125 (credit)

c £145 (overdrawn), −£135, £245, £30 (credit), £57 (overdrawn)

Learn 2 Adding and subtracting negative integers

Examples:

a What is the value of +1 + +4

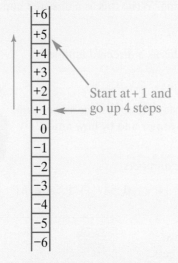

c What is the value of 3 + −2?

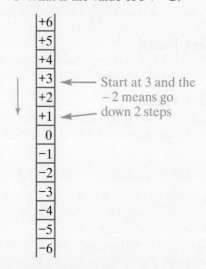

b What is the value of −5 + +6

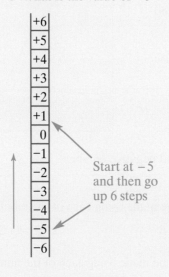

d What is the value of −2 − −4?

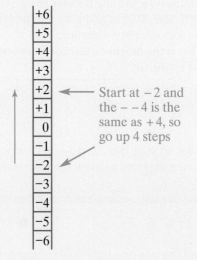

Apply 2

1 Copy this addition table. Starting at the top right-hand corner, calculate $A + B$ and fill in the boxes.
Use the patterns you find to complete the table.

B

	$A + B$	−4	−3	−2	−1	0	+1	+2	+3	+4
	+4									
	+3									
	+2									
	+1									
A	0									
	−1									
	−2									
	−3									
	−4									

2 Find the missing number in each of the following.

a $+3 + ... = +5$

b $+3 + ... = 0$

c $-1 + ... = -3$

d $-2 + ... = -1$

e $4 + ... = -9$

f $... + 1 = -3$

3 What must be added to:

a -4 to make 6?

b 2 to make -2?

c 13 to make 3?

4 Andrew says that $-3 + 5 = -8$. Is he correct? Explain your answer.

5 Copy this subtraction table. Starting at the top right-hand corner, calculate $A - B$ and fill in the boxes.
Use the patterns you find to complete the table.

B

	$A - B$	−4	−3	−2	−1	0	+1	+2	+3	+4
	+4									
	+3									
	+2									
	+1									
A	0									
	−1									
	−2									
	−3									
	−4									

6 Find the missing number in each of the following.

a $+3 - ... = +1$

b $+4 - ... = +5$

c $-3 - ... = -2$

d $-1 - ... = 2$

e $-3 - ... = 0$

f $... - -2 = 3$

7 What must be subtracted from:

    a 14 to make 7   **b** -2 to make -9 **c** -6 to make -3?

8 Get Real!

    a If the temperature is $+3°C$ and it falls by $9°C$, what is the new temperature?

    b If the temperature is $-6°C$, by how many degrees must it rise to become $6°C$?

    c After rising $9°C$ the temperature is $+3°C$. What was it originally?

9 a Fill in the boxes so that the answer to each question is 12.

    i $\quad 15 - \boxed{} = 12$ **iii** $\quad -2 + \boxed{} = 12$

    ii $\quad \boxed{} + -6 = 12$ **iv** $\quad \boxed{} - +8 = 12$

    b Make up five more addition and subtraction questions that have 12 as an answer. You must use negative and positive numbers in each question.

Learn 3   Multiplying and dividing negative integers

Examples: Work out the answers to the following questions.

    a $+2 \times +3$ **c** $-2 \times +3$ **e** $-12 \div +4$

    b $+2 \times -3$ **d** -2×-3 **f** $-6 \div -3$

    a $+2 \times +3$ ⟵ Remember that $+2 \times +3$ **Signs the same = positive**
       $= +6$ is the same as 2×3

    b $+2 \times -3$ ⟵ This is the same as 2×-3 **Signs different = negative**
       $= -6$

    c $-2 \times +3$ ⟵ This is the same as -2×3 **Signs different = negative**
       $= -6$

    d -2×-3 ⟵ Not -6 **Signs the same = positive**
       $= +6$

    e $-12 \div +4$ ⟵ The same rules apply as for multiplication
       $= -3$ **Signs different = negative**

    f $-6 \div -3$ ⟵ The same rules apply as for multiplication
       $= 2$ **Signs the same = positive**

Apply 3

1 Copy the multiplication table. Starting at the top right-hand corner, calculate $A \times B$ and fill in the boxes.
Use the patterns you find to complete the table.

$A \times B$	−4	−3	−2	−1	0	+1	+2	+3	+4
+4									
+3									
+2									
+1									
0									
−1									
−2									
−3									
−4									

B is labelled above the table. *A* is labelled to the left of the table.

2 Find the missing number in each of the following:

a $+3 \times \ldots = +15$ d $-2 \times \ldots = -12$ g $-16 \div \ldots = -4$

b $+3 \times \ldots = -30$ e $4 \times \ldots = -36$ h $\ldots \div -4 = -8$

c $-1 \times \ldots = -3$ f $\ldots \times -10 = 30$ i $\ldots \div -2 = 8$

3 Find the values of these:

a $\dfrac{-2 \times +9}{-3}$ b $\dfrac{16 \times -3}{+4}$ c $\dfrac{-6 \times -7}{-2}$

4 The answer is 24. Can you make up ten questions, involving multiplication and division, that give that answer? You must use negative numbers.

5 Grace has been asked to write down the first five terms of a sequence which starts with 1. The rule for finding the next number is 'multiply the last number by -2'. She writes:

   1   -2 -4 -8 -16

Is she correct? Explain your answer.

6 Find

a two numbers whose sum is -8 and whose product is 15

b two numbers whose sum is -1 and whose product is -20.

Explore

◎ What happens if you keep multiplying negative numbers?

◎ For example, multiply two negative numbers, the answer is positive

◎ Multiply three negative numbers, the answer is ...

Investigate further

Learn 4   Factors and multiples

Examples: **a** What are the factors of 28?

1   2   4   7   14   28

In most cases factors are in pairs
$1 \times 28 = 28$
$2 \times 14 = 28$
$4 \times 7 = 28$

b What are the first five multiples of 4?

4   8   12   16   20

All of the numbers are in the four times table

c What is the least common multiple (LCM) of 6 and 8?

6   12   18   24   30 ← These numbers are all multiples of 6

8   16   24   32   40 ← These numbers are all multiples of 8

The LCM of 6 and 8 is 24.

24 is the smallest number that is common to both lists

d What is the highest common factor (HCF) of 16 and 24?

1   2   4   8   16 ← These numbers are all factors of 16

1   2   3   4   6   8   12   24 ← These numbers are all factors of 24

1   2   4   8 ← 1, 2, 4, 8 are common factors of 16 and 24

The HCF of 16 and 24 is 8.

8 is the highest number that is common to both lists

Apply 4

1 From this set of numbers

2   3   4   5   6   7   8   9

write down the numbers that are factors of:

a 6   **c** 4   **e** 25

b 9   **d** 16   **f** 24

2 Write down all the factors of:

a 15   **c** 48   **e** 40   **g** 32   **i** 84

b 64   **d** 10   **f** 36   **h** 72

3 Find the common factors of:

a 6 and 15   **c** 4 and 64   **e** 25 and 40

b 9 and 48   **d** 10 and 16   **f** 24 and 36

4 Find the HCF of the following sets of numbers.

a 6 and 15   **d** 24 and 36   **g** 84 and 70

b 12 and 15   **e** 27 and 36

c 32 and 48   **f** 56 and 152

5 Write down all the factors of 20 and 24. Hence find the common factors and write down the HCF of 20 and 24.

6 The HCF of two numbers is 5. Give five possible pairs of numbers.

7 Write down the first five multiples of:

a 2	**c** 7	**e** 9	**g** 11	**i** 13
b 5	**d** 6	**f** 12	**h** 8	

8 Find the LCM of these sets of numbers.

a 6 and 15	**d** 3 and 8	**g** 3, 5 and 6
b 12 and 6	**e** 4 and 6	**h** 6, 8 and 32
c 5 and 7	**f** 4, 10 and 12	

9 Get Real!
A lighthouse flashes every 56 seconds. Another lighthouse flashes every 40 seconds. At 9 p.m. they both flash at the same time. What time will it be when they next both flash at the same time?

10 Get Real!
Alison is making her own birthday cards. She needs to cut up lengths of ribbon. Find the smallest length of ribbon that can be cut into an exact number of either 5 cm or 8 cm or 12 cm lengths.

11 Get Real!
One political party holds its annual conference at Eastbourne every four years. Another holds its annual conference there every six years. They both held their conference in Eastbourne in 2006. When will they next be there in the same year?

12 Get Real!
A rectangular floor measures 450 cm by 350 cm. What is the largest square tile that can be used to cover the floor without any cutting?

13 Get Real!
Rectangular tiles measure 15 cm by 9 cm. What is the length of the side of the smallest square area that can be covered with these tiles?

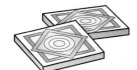

Explore

◎ Write down all the numbers between 1 and 30

◎ Work out the number of factors for each number

◎ Can you work out a rule for numbers that have

    a two factors only

    b an odd number of factors?

> **Investigate further**

Learn 5   Prime numbers and prime factor decomposition

Example:

Find the prime factors of 40.

Start by finding the smallest prime number that divides into 40.
Continue dividing by successive prime numbers until the answer becomes 1.

2	40
2	20
2	10
5	5
	1

Prime numbers are numbers with exactly two factors, for example, 2, 3, 5, 7, 11, 13, ...

The prime factors of 40 are 2, 2, 2, 5.
40 written as a product of prime factors is $2 \times 2 \times 2 \times 5$.
This can be written as $2^3 \times 5$.

This is called 'index notation'.
The index tells you how many times the factor 2 occurs

Apply 5

1 Write each of the following numbers as a product of prime factors.

   a 20   **c** 36   **e** 90   **g** 63   **i** 84

   b 18   **d** 66   **f** 100   **h** 48   **j** 96

2 Express each number as a product of its prime factors.

   a 24   **b** 72   **c** 45

3 Express each number as a product of its prime factors.
   Write your answers using index notation.

   a 220   **c** 136   **e** 720   **g** 390   **i** 624

   b 144   **d** 300   **f** 480   **h** 450   **j** 216

4 Clare says that one must be a prime number. Is she correct? Explain your answer.

5 What number is this?

   a It is less than 100, it is 1 less than a multiple of 7, it is a prime number and
   its digits add up to 5.

   b It is less than 100, it is a multiple of 11 and it is 2 more than a square number.
   If it is divided by 9 there is a remainder of 3.

6 Write 2420 as a product of its prime factors. Write your answer using index notation.

7 Write 9240 as a product of its prime factors. Write your answer using index notation.

8 Write 8820 as a product of its prime factors. Write your answer using index notation.

Explore

You will need a 100 square

◎ Cross out the number 1

◎ Put a circle round the number 2 and then cross out all of the other multiples of 2

◎ Put a circle round the next number after 2 which has not been crossed out

◎ Cross out all of the other multiples of that number

◎ Put a circle round the next number not crossed out and cross out every multiple of that number

◎ Continue until you run out of numbers in the 100 square

What do you notice about the numbers that are left?

Investigate further

Learn 6   Reciprocals

Examples: Find the reciprocal of: **a** 5   **b** $\frac{1}{4}$ **c** 0.3   **d** $2\frac{1}{2}$

a The reciprocal of 5 is $\frac{1}{5}$ ⟵———————— You can write 5 as $\frac{5}{1}$

The reciprocal of $\frac{5}{1}$ is $\frac{1}{5}$

b The reciprocal of $\frac{1}{4}$ is $\frac{4}{1} = 4$ ⟵———— It is better to write $\frac{4}{1}$ as 4

c The reciprocal of 0.3 is the same as ⟵———— Write 0.3 as a fraction
the reciprocal of $\frac{3}{10}$

The reciprocal of $\frac{3}{10}$ is $\frac{10}{3} = 3\frac{1}{3}$ ⟵———— It is better to write $\frac{10}{3}$ as $3\frac{1}{3}$

d The reciprocal of $2\frac{1}{2}$ is the same as ⟵———— Write $2\frac{1}{2}$ as $\frac{5}{2}$
the reciprocal of $\frac{5}{2}$

The reciprocal of $\frac{5}{2}$ is $\frac{2}{5}$

Apply 6

 1 Write down the reciprocal of

    a 4   **b** 6   **c** 8   **d** 10   **e** 7   **f** 0.25

 2 Find the reciprocal of

    a $\frac{1}{2}$ **b** $\frac{1}{5}$ **c** $\frac{1}{7}$ **d** $\frac{1}{8}$ **e** $\frac{1}{12}$ **f** 0.8

3 Find the reciprocal of

    a $\frac{2}{7}$ **b** $\frac{3}{5}$ **c** $\frac{2}{3}$ **d** $\frac{5}{6}$ **e** 0.125   **f** $0.\dot{3}$

4 Find the reciprocal of

    a $2\frac{1}{4}$ **b** $3\frac{1}{2}$ **c** $1\frac{3}{4}$ **d** 1.25   **e** 3.6   **f** $1.\dot{6}$

5 Find the reciprocals of the numbers 2 to 12, as decimals. If they are not exact, write them as recurring decimals. Which of the numbers have reciprocals that

    a are exact decimals

    b have one recurring figure

    c have two recurring figures?

Explore

◉ Write down the reciprocals of $2, 1, \frac{1}{2}, \frac{1}{4}, \frac{1}{8}, \ldots$

◉ Continue the pattern

◉ What do you notice?

Investigate further

Integers

ASSESS

The following exercise tests your understanding of this chapter, with the questions appearing in order of increasing difficulty.

1 In a magic square each number is different. The sum of each row, each column and each diagonal is the same. Fill in the missing numbers in the magic square.

−1	−2	
	0	−4
	2	

2 In a magic square each number is different. The sum of each row, each column and each diagonal is the same.

	−9	−2	1	12
9	5	−6	7	
−10	4	2	0	14
	−3	10	−1	−7
−8		6		−4

    a Fill in the missing numbers.

    b What is the sum of any row, column or diagonal?

This magic square has a smaller magic square inside it.

    c Find this magic square.

    d What is the sum of each of its diagonals, rows and columns?

3 Copy and complete the following table.

Temperature	Change	New temperature
4	+5	
4	−7	
−2	+6	
−1	−4	
13		22
24		1
1		−3
−2		−4
	+4	7
	+13	9
	−11	−2
	−7	2

4 Julius Sneezar was born in the year 25 BC and his wife, Bigga, in 21 BC.
Julius died in AD 33 and Bigga in AD 41.
Assume that they had each had their birthdays in the year they died.

   a How old was Julius when he died?

   b How old was Bigga when she died?

5 Find the values of each of these.

   a 2×-5 **d** -4×0 **g** $-45 \div -15$

   b -6×7 **e** $16 \div -4$ **h** $0 \div -2$

   c -8×-3 **f** $-24 \div 2$

6 Write down the first six terms of the sequence that starts with 100
and where each term is the previous term divided by -2.

7 At a party it was discovered that Siobhan, Gareth, Nathan and Ulrika had
birthdays on the 6th, 15th, 27th and 30th of the month. Sven joined the
group and it was discovered that his birthday was a factor of everyone else's.
If Sven was not born on the 1st, on what day of the month was Sven born?

8 Find the prime factors of: **a** 420   **b** 13 475

9 Find the reciprocals of:

   a 5   **c** $\frac{5}{8}$ **e** $0.\dot{2}$

   b -8 **d** -0.2

10 a What is the only number that is the same as its reciprocal?

   b What is the only number that has no reciprocal?
   Explain your answer.

Try some real past exam questions to test your knowledge:

11 Tom, Sam and Matt are counting drum beats.

Tom hits a snare drum every 2 beats.
Sam hits a kettle drum every 5 beats.
Matt hits a bass drum every 8 beats.

Tom, Sam and Matt start by hitting their drums at the same time.
How many beats is it before Tom, Sam and Matt **next** hit their drums at the
same time?

Spec A, Higher Paper 1, June 04

12 a Express 144 as the product of its prime factors.
Write your answer in index form.

b Find the highest common factor (HCF) of 60 and 144.

Spec B, Mod 3 Intermediate, June 03

2 Rounding

G **Examiners would normally expect students who get a G grade to be able to:**

Round to the nearest integer

Write an integer correct to the nearest 10 or the nearest 100

Estimate answers to problems involving decimals

F **Examiners would normally expect students who get an F grade also to be able to:**

Estimate square roots

Round numbers to given powers of 10 and to a given number of decimal places

E **Examiners would normally expect students who get an E grade also to be able to:**

Round a number to one significant figure

D **Examiners would normally expect students who get a D grade also to be able to:**

Estimate answers to calculations such as $\dfrac{22.6 \times 18.7}{5.2}$

C **Examiners would normally expect students who get a C grade also to be able to:**

Estimate answers to calculations such as $\dfrac{22.6 \times 18.7}{0.52}$

Find minimum and maximum values

What you should already know ...

■ Arrange whole numbers and decimal numbers in order of size

■ Work with number lines

VOCABULARY

Round – give an approximate value of a number; numbers can be rounded to the nearest 1000, nearest 100, nearest 10, nearest integer, significant figures, decimal places, ... etc.

Significant figures – the digits in a number; the closer a digit is to the beginning of a number then the more important or significant it is; for example, in the number 23.657, 2 is the most significant digit and is worth 20, 7 is the least significant digit and is worth $\frac{7}{1000}$; the number 23.657 has 5 significant digits

Decimal places – the digits to the right of a decimal point in a number, for example, in the number 23.657, the number 6 is the first decimal place (worth $\frac{6}{10}$), the number 5 is the second decimal place (worth $\frac{5}{100}$) and 7 is the third decimal place (worth $\frac{7}{1000}$); the number 23.657 has 3 decimal places

Estimate – find an approximate value of a calculation; this is usually found by rounding all of the numbers to one significant figure, for example, $\frac{20.4 \times 4.3}{5.2}$ is approximately $\frac{20 \times 4}{5}$ where each number is rounded to 1 s.f., the answer can be worked out in your head to give 16

Upper bound – this is the maximum possible value of a measurement, for example, if a length is measured as 37 cm correct to the nearest centimetre, the upper bound of the length is 37.5 cm

Lower bound – this is the minimum possible value of a measurement, for example, if a length is measured as 37 cm correct to the nearest centimetre, the lower bound of the length is 36.5 cm

Learn 1 Rounding numbers and quantities

Example: Round 63 and 48 to the nearest 10.

To the nearest 10, all these numbers round to 60

The number 65 rounds up to 70

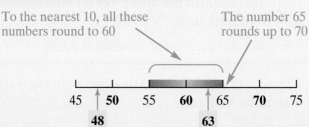

All numbers between 55 and 65 round to 60 to the nearest 10, because they are nearer to 60 than they are to 50 or 70.

So 63 rounded to the nearest 10 is 60.

48 is nearer to 50 than 40, so 48 rounded to the nearest 10 is 50.

Apply 1

1

Round these to the nearest whole number.
(The number line may help to get you started.)

a 7.6   **b** 5.2   **c** 67.8   **d** 0.8   **e** 0.2   **f** 89.5

2 Round these numbers   **a** to the nearest 10   **b** to the nearest 100.

i 166   **ii** 234   **iii** 2022   **iv** 1598   **v** 16.1   **vi** 245

3 Round the numbers in question **2** to the nearest 5.

4 a Hannah says that 3284 rounded to the nearest 100 is 33.
What has she done wrong?

   b Sanjay says that 7.6 rounded to the nearest whole number is 8.0
What mistake has he made?

5 Here is some incorrect rounding. Write a corrected statement in each case.

   a 416 291 rounds to 4163

   b 2997 to the nearest 10 is 2990

   c 54.8 to the nearest whole number is 55.0

6 Draw a number line marked with numbers from 0 to 5 and colour the part of the line

   a containing all the numbers that round to 3 when rounded to the nearest whole number

   b containing all the numbers that round to 1.4 when rounded to the nearest tenth.

7 Write down four different 4-digit numbers that

   a become 9300 when rounded to the nearest 100

   b become 9300 when rounded to the nearest 50.

   c Which of your numbers could be the answers to both parts **a** and **b**?

8 Get Real!

What is the length of this pencil   **a** to the nearest centimetre   **b** to the nearest half centimetre
c to the nearest 5 centimetres   **d** to the nearest 10 centimetres?

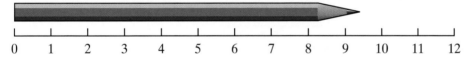

9 Aled's height is 148 cm. What is this to the nearest 10 cm? To the nearest half metre?

10 Round these amounts of money   **a** to the nearest pound   **b** to the nearest 50 pence.

   i £54.64   **ii** £1.73   **iii** £235.24   **iv** 84 pence   **v** £0.34

11 An amount of money correct to the nearest pound is £52.
What is the largest amount it could be? What is the smallest?

12 The number of people at a concert is 7000 to the nearest 1000 people.
What is the smallest possible number of people at the concert?

13 The number of spectators at a football match was 34 485.
A local newspaper reported this as 35 000.
Was this correct? Give a reason for your answer.

Explore

◎ Mathematicians and statisticians don't always round numbers like 15.5 and 4.5 up to the next whole number above

◎ Instead, they round up or down to make the number **even** – so 15.5 rounds to 16 and 4.5 rounds to 4

◎ Why might this be a good idea?

Investigate further

Learn 2 Rounding to significant figures and decimal places

Examples:

a Round the following numbers to:

i one significant figure   **ii** two significant figures.

3456   345.6   34.56   3.456   0.3456   0.03456   0.003456

Number	One significant figure	Two significant figures
3456	3000	3500
345.5	300	350
34.56	30	35
3.456	3	3.5
0.3456	0.3	0.35
0.03456	0.03	0.035
0.003456	0.003	0.0035

Zeros are not significant figures. They are used to pad out the number to make it the correct size

3.456 is closer to 3.5 than 3.4 when written to one significant figure

The number 3 is the most significant figure when rounding to one significant figure

The numbers 3 and 5 are the most significant figures when rounding to two significant figures

b Round the following numbers to:

i one decimal place   **ii** two decimal places.

34.56   3.456   0.3456   0.03456   0.003456

Number	One decimal place	Two decimal places
34.56	34.6	34.56
3.456	3.5	3.46
0.3456	0.3	0.35
0.03456	0.0	0.03
0.003456	0.0	0.00

3.456 is closer to 3.5 than 3.4 when written to one decimal place

0.3456 is closer to 0.35 than 0.34 when written to two decimal places

In this example the answers contain only one decimal place

In this example the answers contain only two decimal places

Apply 2

1 Round these   **a** to one significant figure   **b** to two significant figures.

i 166   **ii** 234   **iii** 2022   **iv** 1598   **v** 16.1   **vi** 245

2 Round these   **a** to one significant figure   **b** to two significant figures.

i 3.78   **ii** 0.378   **iii** 0.0526   **iv** 0.00526   **v** 0.000526   **vi** 0.0000526

3 Round the numbers in question **2** to two decimal places.

4 Get Real!
Round these amounts of money to two decimal places
(that is, to the nearest penny).

a £19.257   **b** £25.387   **c** £235.24   **d** £25.397   **e** £0.5621

5 Round these measurements to one decimal place (that is, to the nearest millimetre).

    a 24.67 cm   **b** 4.93 cm   **c** 73.45 cm   **d** 0.566 cm   **e** 0.5454 cm

6 Round these weights to three decimal places (that is, to the nearest gram).

    a 1.5396 kg   **b** 41.733 kg   **c** 5.9863 kg   **d** 0.045365 kg   **e** 0.0008454 kg

Explore

◎ Find a number that is the same when rounded to the nearest whole number as to one significant figure

◎ Find a number that is the same when rounded to the nearest 10 as to one significant figure

◎ Find a number that is the same when rounded to one decimal place as to one significant figure

◎ Find a number that is the same when rounded to two decimal places as to one significant figure

Investigate further

Learn 3   Estimating

Example:

Estimate the answer to 3.86×2.14

Round all the numbers to one significant figure, then work out the approximate answer in your head.

3.86 is 4 to one significant figure ⟶ 3.86×2.14 ⟵ 2.14 is 2 to one significant figure

$$3.86 \times 2.14 \approx 4 \times 2 = 8$$

This curly equals sign means 'is approximately equal to'

It is easy to make mistakes when using decimals, so it is a good idea to estimate to find the approximate size of the answer so that you can see if you are right.

Apply 3

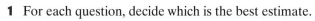

1 For each question, decide which is the best estimate.

		Estimate A	Estimate B	Estimate C
a	2.89×9.4	2.7	18	27
b	1.2×29.4	3	30	300
c	$9.17 \div 3.2$	3	4	18
d	48.5×9.8	5	50	500
e	$4.2 \div 1.9$	1	2	3
f	22.4×6.1	12	120	180
g	$7.8 \div 1.2$	8	78	80
h	$2.1 \times 3.1 \div 4.2$	1	1.5	2
i	$20.9 \div 6.9 \times 4.1$	10	11	12

2 Estimate the answers to these calculations by rounding to one significant figure. You may wish to use a calculator to check your answers.

a $2.9 + 3.2$

b $7.9 \div 2.2$

c $67.8 + 22.1$

d $\dfrac{20.4 \times 7.7}{5.2}$

e 0.2×5.4

f $4.3 - 3.7$

g 5.3×8.2

h $\dfrac{20.4 \times 7.7}{0.52}$

i $\dfrac{75.5 \times 2.7}{0.12}$

j $\dfrac{28.5 + 53}{64.1 - 53.7}$

k $\dfrac{102.4 + 8.7}{0.22}$

l $\dfrac{102.4 \times 8.7}{0.22}$

m $21.3(7.56 + 3.89)$

n $21.3(7.56 - 3.89)$

> **HINT** Be careful when dividing by numbers less than one.

3 For each pair of calculations, estimate the answers to help decide which you think will have the bigger answer. Use a calculator to check your answers.

a 5.2×1.8 or 3.1×2.95

b $28.4 \div 5.9$ or 2.03×3.78

c $9.723 + 4.28$ or $39.4 \div 2.04$

d 39.5×21.3 or 81.3×7.8

4 The square root of 10 lies between the square root of 9 and the square root of 16. The square root of 9 is 3 and the square root of 16 is 4, so the answer lies between 3 and 4.

Use this method to estimate the square root of:

a 12   **b** 20   **c** 50   **d** 3   **e** 1000

5 Estimate 5.92×3.82 by rounding to the nearest whole number. Explain why the answer is an over-estimate of the exact answer.

6 Sam says, 'I estimated the answer to $16.7 - 8.6$ as 8 by rounding up both numbers, so the answer is an over-estimate.' Show that Sam is not correct.

7 Ali says, '35 divided by 5 is 7, so 35 divided by 0.5 is 0.7'. Is Ali right? Give a reason for your answer.

8 Give one example that shows that dividing can make something smaller and another to show that dividing can make something bigger.

9 Hannah says:

- When I rounded the numbers in a calculation I got $\frac{110}{0.2}$

- Then I multiplied the top and the bottom both by 10 to give $\frac{1100}{2}$

- So the answer is 550.

Is Hannah correct? Give a reason for your answer.

10 a Find five numbers whose square roots are between 7 and 8.

    b Find two consecutive whole numbers to complete this statement: 'The square root of 60 is between ... and ...'

11 Get Real!
Estimate the total cost of three books costing £3.99, £5.25 and £10.80

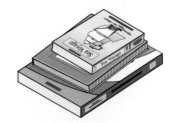

12 Get Real!

Estimate the length of fencing needed for this field.

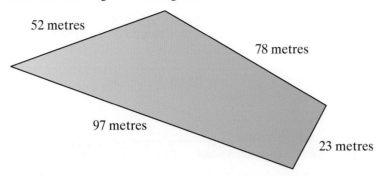

52 metres

78 metres

97 metres

23 metres

13 Get Real!

Anne's car goes 6.2 miles on every litre of petrol. Estimate how far she can drive if her fuel tank has 24.5 litres in it.

14 Get Real!

A group of 18 people wins £389 540 on the lottery. Estimate how much each person will get when the money is shared out equally.

15 Get Real!

It's Harry's birthday! He asks his mum for a cake like a football pitch. She makes a cake that is 29 cm wide and 38 cm long.

a She wants to put a ribbon round the cake. She can buy ribbon in various lengths: 1 m, 1.5 m, 2 m, 2.5 m or 3 m.
Estimate the perimeter of the cake and say which length ribbon she should buy.

b She can buy ready-made green icing for the top of the cake. The icing comes in packs to cover 1000 cm^2.
Estimate the area of the top of the cake and decide whether one pack will be enough.

Explore

◎ You know that $20 \times 30 = 600$
So the answers to all these calculations will be close to 600, as the numbers are close to 20×30:

a 19.4×28.7 **d** 21.2×30.4 **g** 23.4×33.4
b 23.4×30.2 **e** 29.8×20.4 **h** 22.3×29.8
c 18.8×29.6 **f** 31.4×18.7

◎ Can you decide which answers will be less than 600, and which will be more than 600?

◎ Check your predictions with a calculator

◎ When can you be sure an estimate is lower than the actual answer?

◎ When can you be sure an estimate is higher than the actual answer?

Investigate further

Learn 4   Finding minimum and maximum values

Example: The length of a table is measured as 60 cm, correct to the nearest centimetre. What are the minimum and maximum possible lengths of the table?

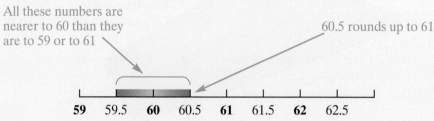

All these numbers are nearer to 60 than they are to 59 or to 61

60.5 rounds up to 61

59   59.5   **60**   60.5   **61**   61.5   **62**   62.5

Any length given to the nearest centimetre could be up to half a centimetre smaller or larger than the given value

A length given to the nearest centimetre as 60 cm could be anything between 59.5 cm and 60.5 cm. The minimum and maximum possible lengths are 59.5 cm and 60.5 cm or $59.5 \leqslant x < 60.5$

The length cannot actually be 60.5 cm, as this measurement rounds up to 61 cm – but it can be as close to 60.5 cm as you like, so 60.5 cm is the top limit (or **upper bound**) of the length

Apply 4

1 Each of these quantities is rounded to the nearest whole number of units. Write down the minimum and maximum possible size of each quantity.

   a 54 cm   **d** 17 mℓ

   b 5 kg   **e** £45

   c 26 m   **f** 175 g

2 Jane says,

   'If a length is 78 cm to the nearest centimetre, then the maximum possible length is 78.49 cm.'

   Is Jane right? Explain your answer.

3 The volume of water in a tank is given as 1500 litres.

   a Decide if the volume has been rounded to the nearest litre, nearest 10 litres or nearest 100 litres if the minimum possible volume is:

      i 1450 ℓ **ii** 1499.5 ℓ **iii** 1495 ℓ

   b If the actual volume is V litres, complete this statement in each case: ... $\leqslant V < $ ....

   c Explain why there is a 'less than or equal to' sign before the V but a 'less than' sign after the V.

   d How do you know that a volume written as 1500 litres has not been measured to the nearest tenth of a litre?

4 Get Real!

ChocoBars should weigh 40 grams with a tolerance of 5% either way.
If the bars weigh 40 grams correct to the nearest 10 grams, will they be
within the tolerance? Show how you worked out your answer.
Why do you think that manufacturers have a 'tolerance' in the sizes of their
products?

5 Get Real!

What is the maximum possible total weight of 10 cartons, each weighing
1.4 kg correct to the nearest 100 g?
Why might someone need to do a calculation like this in real life?

Explore

 Write a note to explain to someone else how to find the minimum and
maximum possible ages of a person whose age is given as a whole number
of years, for example, 8 years

 Write a note to explain to someone else how to find the minimum and
maximum possible amounts of money when the quantity is given to the
nearest pound, for example, £18

Investigate further

Rounding

ASSESS

The following exercise tests your understanding of this chapter,
with the questions appearing in order of increasing difficulty.

1 4645 people watch Redruth win their latest match.
Write this number

   a to the nearest 1000   **c** to the nearest 50

   b to the nearest 100   **d** to the nearest 10.

2 Copy and complete the table below.

Starting number	To the nearest 10	To the nearest 500	To the nearest 1000
66 329	66 330		
206 021			206 000
211 372		211 500	
332 404			
852 612			

3 The square root of 200 is bigger than one integer (whole number) and
smaller than another.

   a What are these two integers?

   b Looking at the square of these two numbers, what is the square root of
200 to the nearest integer?

4 The world's tallest person was Robert Wadlow who died in 1840. He measured 271.78 cm (8 ft 11 in). The shortest adult male was Calvin Phillips who died in 1812. He measured 67.31 cm (2 ft $2\frac{1}{2}$ in).

Write both these metric heights to one decimal place.

5 Round the five numbers in question **2** to one significant figure.

6 Gary says that he and Jane are the same age – to one significant figure. Gary is 44 and Jane is 36. Is Gary correct? Explain your answer.

7 The average person's heart beats about once a second. Estimate how many times it beats during a year.

8 The (movement) energy of an athlete of mass 43 kg running at a velocity of 9.7 m/s can be found by working out $43 \times 9.7 \times 9.7 \div 2$. Use appropriate approximations for 43 and 9.7 and estimate the athlete's energy.

9 Ngugi lives on the equator, which is a circle of diameter 12 756 km. George lives in the UK on a circle of latitude with diameter 7854 km. To calculate the distance each boy moves in one day due to the Earth's rotation we multiply each diameter by 3.14

Write all three values given above correct to **the nearest thousand** and hence estimate how much further Ngugi travels than George in one day.

10 Estimate the value of: **a** $\dfrac{9.6^2 - 4.2^2}{2 \times 9.65}$ **b** $\dfrac{24.8 \times 3.2}{0.54}$

11 a The length of a rectangle is given as 27 m correct to the nearest m. Write down the minimum and maximum possible lengths it could be.

  b A different length is given as 5.0 cm correct to the nearest mm. Write down the minimum and maximum possible lengths it could be.

Try a real past exam question to test your knowledge:

12 a Work out 600×0.3

  b Work out $600 \div 0.3$

  c You are told that $432 \times 21 = 9072$
  Write down the value of $9072 \div 2.1$

  d Find an approximate value of $\dfrac{2987}{21 \times 49}$
  You **must** show all your working.

Spec A, Int Paper 1, Nov 03

3 Decimals

OBJECTIVES

 F

Examiners would normally expect students who get an F grade to be able to:

Write down the place value of a digit such as the value of the 4 in 0.24

Order decimals, for example, which is bigger, 0.24 or 0.3?

E

Examiners would normally expect students who get an E grade also to be able to:

Add and subtract decimals

 D

Examiners would normally expect students who get a D grade also to be able to:

Multiply two decimals such as 2.4×0.7

Convert decimals to fractions and fractions to decimals

C

Examiners would normally expect students who get a C grade also to be able to:

Divide a number by a decimal such as $1 \div 0.2$ and $2.8 \div 0.07$

What you should already know ...

■ Add, subtract, multiply and divide whole numbers

VOCABULARY

Digit – any of the numerals from 0 to 9

Integer – any positive or negative whole number or zero, for example, $-2, -1, 0, 1, 2, ...$

Decimal – a number in which a decimal point separates the whole number part from the decimal part, for example, 24.8

Numerator – the number on the top of a fraction

Numerator $\longrightarrow \dfrac{3}{8} \longleftarrow$ Denominator

Denominator – the number on the bottom of a fraction

Terminating decimal – a decimal that ends, for example, 0.3, 0.33 or 0.3333

Recurring decimal – a decimal with a repeating digit or group of digits, for example, 0.33333333333 ... (written as 0.3̇) or 0.25678678678678 ... (written as 0.25̇67̇8̇)

Learn 1 Place value

The decimal point separates the whole numbers from the fractions.

12	.	345
Whole numbers	.	Fractions

Examples:

a What is the value of the 2 in 0.425?

Write out the number with the headings.

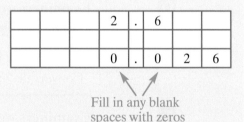

Thousands	Hundreds	Tens	Units	.	Tenths	Hundredths	Thousandths
			0	.	4	2	5

The value of 2 is 2 hundredths.

b Calculate 2.6 ÷ 100.

Remember the digits move one place for each 0 – one place for 10, two for 100, three for 1000, ...

			2	.	6		
			0	.	0	2	6

2.6 ÷ 100 = 0.026

Fill in any blank spaces with zeros

Apply 1

1 Put these numbers in order of size, starting with the smallest.

2.4   3   2.06   2.175   1.999   0.987

2 Write down the value of the digit 5 in each of these numbers.

a 3.5   **c** 5.34   **e** 1.235   **g** 2.514

b 2.45   **d** 0.156   **f** 523.46   **h** 5432.1

3 Bronwyn says that 2.4 × 10 is 2.40.
What has she done wrong?

4 Write down the answers to these questions.

a 2.4 × 10   **c** 5 ÷ 10   **e** 4.5 × 100   **g** 4.2 × 100 ÷ 10

b 4.2 × 1000   **d** 3.2 ÷ 1000   **f** 0.02 ÷ 1000   **h** 2 ÷ 100 × 10

5 How many lots of 0.2 make 200?

6 Get Real!

The Healthy Bite Café serves 1000 drinks of orange juice every day. The staff serve the drinks in cups containing 0.3 litres of orange juice. They charge £0.85 for each cup.

a How many litres of orange juice do they sell in a day?

b How much money do they take for the sales of orange juice?

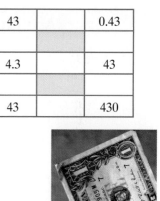

7 The grid below gives correct calculations from left to right and top to bottom. (Every blue arrow shows a correct calculation).

For example, 2 ÷ 10 = 0.2

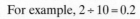

For example, 2 × 10 = 20

2	÷ 10	0.2	× 1000	200
× 10		÷ 10		÷ 100
20	÷ 1000	0.02	× 100	2
÷ 100		× 10 000		× 10
0.2	× 1000	200	÷ 10	20

Copy these grids and fill in the gaps in the same way.

4.2	÷ 10		× 100	
× 10		÷ 10		÷ 100
	÷ 1000		× 10	
÷ 100		× 100		× 100
	× 10		× 10	

4.3		43		0.43
430		4.3		43
4.3		43		430

8 £1 is worth $1.84

a How many dollars is £10 worth?

b How many dollars is £1000 worth?

9 Niranjan puts a number into his calculator. He then performs these calculations:

× 100 ÷ 10 ÷ 100 × 1000 ÷ 10

His calculator gives an answer of 23.4 – with what number did he start?

10 a Can you find the correct route through this maze? You can only move horizontally or vertically, onto a square with the correct answer.

Start	3.4 × 10 = 34	2.7 × 100 = 2.700	30.8 ÷ 100 = 0.308	51.2 – 10 = 41.2	1.09 ÷ 100 = 0.0109
3.4 × 10 = 0.34	42 ÷ 100 = 0.42	12.4 – 10 = 2.4	0.2 ÷ 100 = 0.002	14.5 ÷ 10 = 0.145	3 ÷ 1000 = 0.003
2.1 × 100 = 21	2.7 × 10 = 20.7	4 ÷ 100 = 0.40	3 ÷ 10 = 30	0.7 × 100 = 700	0.2 ÷ 100 = 0.002
0.1 × 100 = 10	20 ÷ 100 = 0.2	40.9 ÷ 10 = 4.09	20.6 ÷ 10 = 2.6	0.4 × 100 = 40	0.1 × 100 = 10
1.4 + 1 = 2.4	3.2 + 100 = 320	8.03 × 10 = 80.3	6.12 × 100 = 621	1.9 × 1000 = 1900	0.12 × 10 = 0.120
End	15.3 – 10 = 1.53	2 ÷ 1000 = 0.002	1.4 × 10 = 14	0.9 ÷ 100 = 0.009	3.7 ÷ 10 = 0.037

b Now correct the wrong answers.

Explore

Kate says that if you start with any number and run it through this machine chain, you get back to your starting number ...

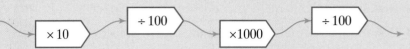

$\times 10$ $\div 100$ $\times 1000$ $\div 100$

Try it and see.

◉ Make up some machine chains of your own that take you back to your starting number – try to find at least two different chains

◉ Make up some chains of different lengths which take you back to the starting number

◉ Make up some chains that do not return to the starting value
Can you predict the effect?

(Investigate further)

Learn 2   Adding and subtracting decimals

Examples: **a** $4.2 + 5.1$ **b** $6.1 - 2.8$ **c** $5.84 + 1.4$ **d** $3.29 - 1.4$ **e** $5.2 - 2.46$

Adding and subtracting decimals is very much like adding and subtracting whole numbers. Just line up the decimal points to make sure you are adding or subtracting digits with the same place value

$$\begin{array}{r} 4.2 \\ +5.1 \\ \hline 9.3 \end{array} \qquad \begin{array}{r} {}^5\!6.{}^1\!1 \\ -2.8 \\ \hline 3.3 \end{array} \qquad \begin{array}{r} 5.84 \\ +1.40 \\ \hline {}_17.24 \end{array} \qquad \begin{array}{r} {}^2\!3.{}^1\!29 \\ -1.40 \\ \hline 1.89 \end{array} \qquad \begin{array}{r} {}^4\!5.{}^{11}\!2{}^1\!0 \\ -2.46 \\ \hline 2.74 \end{array}$$

To avoid mistakes, put 0 in any 'spaces' to make both numbers line up on the right

Apply 2

1 Work these out:

   a $4.2 + 3.7$ **e** $12.1 + 4.9$ **i** $2.345 + 3.456$

   b $1.2 + 8.8$ **f** $2.1 + 4.32$ **j** $2.456 + 4.32$

   c $4.7 + 6.6$ **g** $6.32 + 4.1$ **k** $6.4 + 7.734$

   d $8.23 + 3.56$ **h** $4.3 + 5.97$ **l** $3 + 4.2 + 5.46$

2 Yusef says that $3.2 + 1.34 = 4.36$.
Isaac says $3.2 + 1.34 = 4.54$.
Who is correct?
Give a reason for your answer.

3 Work these out:

a 4.5 – 3.2   **e** 8.1 – 5.9   **i** 7.385 – 4.727

b 6.2 – 1.2   **f** 8.24 – 4.2   **j** 8.345 – 5.61

c 5.7 – 3.9   **g** 7.3 – 3.18   **k** 3.8 – 2.199

d 7.43 – 3.39   **h** 9.3 – 5.86   **l** 4.7 – 1.345

4 Bill says that 4.6 – 1.32 = 3.28
Ted says 4.6 – 1.32 = 3.32
Who made the mistake?
Give a reason for your answer.

5 Work these out:

a 4.2 + 5.1 – 2.8   **d** 2.15 – 1.4 + 3.2   **g** 2.76 – 1.4 – 1.23

b 3.1 – 1.7 + 5.2   **e** 2.4 – 1.23 + 4.56 – 1.2   **h** 9 – 2.34 – 1.8

c 1.9 + 2.42 – 1.6   **f** 6.1 – 4.56 – 1.2   **i** 21.2 – 14.6 + 1.3 – 2.45

6 Fill in the missing numbers (shown as ☺) in these calculations.

a 2.4 + 1.3 = ☺.7   **c** 3.☺ + 2.4 = 5.8   **e** ☺.2 + 4.☺ = 7.1

b 5.4 – 1.2 = ☺.☺   **d** ☺.7 – 2.8 = 2.☺   **f** 9.☺ – 4.2 = ☺.5

7 This question is about the four numbers below.

A	B	C	D
2.4	4.62	6.9	9.16

a Work out **C** + **D**.

b Work out (**A** + **D**) – (**B** + **C**).

c Work out **B** – **A**, **C** – **B**, and **D** – **C**. Use your answers to decide which two numbers are closest together.

d Add your three answers to part **c** together.

e Calculate **D** – **A**. What do you notice?

8 Get Real!

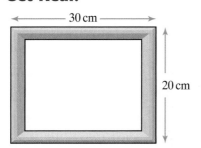

A picture frame measures 30 cm by 20 cm.

Oliver drops it, and it breaks into eight pieces. Here are the measurements of each piece.

4.6 cm	8.6 cm
12.6 cm	15.4 cm
8.6 cm	11.4 cm
17.4 cm	21.4 cm

a Can you put the bits in pairs to rebuild the frame? (You need to make two lengths of 20 cm and two lengths of 30 cm.)

b Can you use the same pieces to make a frame that measures 24 cm by 26 cm instead?

9 The questions below all have the same four numbers in them.

   a Which three of these arrangements have the same answer?

     i $2.4 + 3.73 - 1.6 - 3.2$ **iii** $3.73 - 1.6 + 3.2 - 2.4$ **v** $3.73 + 2.4 - 3.2 - 1.6$

     ii $3.73 - 1.6 + 2.4 - 3.2$ **iv** $3.73 + 1.6 - 2.4 - 3.2$ **vi** $3.2 + 2.4 - 3.73 - 1.6$

   b Why do they have the same answer?

   c Can you use what you have discovered to make these questions easier
     by avoiding going into negative numbers?

     i $4.1 - 5.6 + 3.8$ **iii** $2 - 4.8 + 3.2$

     ii $1.2 - 5 + 6.4$ **iv** $1.2 - 4.56 - 3.1 + 10$

10 Imagine you have three bricks like this one:

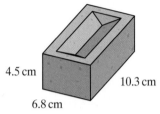

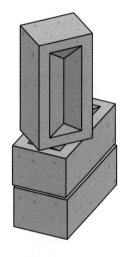

4.5 cm   10.3 cm

6.8 cm

You can put them in a line, you can stack them up,
you can turn them round, ...
What different heights can you make using one, two or all three bricks?

Explore

  ◎   Find two numbers that add up to 9.4 but have a difference of 1.2

  ◎   Find two numbers that add up to 5.3 but have a difference of 1.5

  ◎   Find two numbers that add up to 6.2 but have a difference of 3.1

Is there a quick way to find the numbers?

Investigate further

Explore

Harry has stamps costing £0.27 each, and stamps costing £0.19 each

  ◎   Show how he could use these stamps to post a parcel costing £1.57

  ◎   Which amounts between £1 and £2 can he make exactly?

Investigate further

Learn 3 Multiplying decimals

Example:

Calculate 0.78×5.2

First remove decimal points: 78×52

Then multiply in your usual way
(The grid method is shown here,
but use your usual method.)

×	**70**	**8**
50	3500	400
2	140	16

$$
\begin{array}{r}
3500 \\
400 \\
140 \\
+\quad 16 \\
\hline
4056
\end{array}
$$

Finally, put the decimal point back in the answer.

Estimate that 0.78×5.2 is about $1 \times 5 = 5$.

So $0.78 \times 5.2 = 4.056$

Alternatively, count up the number of decimal places in the question.

There are three decimal places in the question: 0.78×5.2

So you need three decimal places in the answer: 4.056

So $0.78 \times 5.2 = 4.056$

Apply 3

1 Use the multiplication $23 \times 52 = 1196$ to help you to complete the questions.

   a 2.3×52 **d** 0.23×52 **g** 0.023×0.052

   b 2.3×5.2 **e** 0.23×0.52

   c 0.23×5.2 **f** 0.23×0.052

2 Calculate:

   a 0.13×22 **e** 1.7×0.22 **i** 8.7×2.5

   b 1.5×2.3 **f** 3.2×13 **j** 8.9×0.16

   c 0.7×1.3 **g** 5.1×2.3 **k** 73.1×0.12

   d 1.1×4.5 **h** 2.7×0.13 **l** 14.3×2.3

3 Now check your answers in question **2** are correct by estimating.

4 Using your answers to question **2**, write down the answers to these.

   a 1.3×22 **e** 17×2.2 **i** 0.087×0.025

   b 1.5×0.23 **f** 0.032×13 **j** 0.0089×0.016

   c 0.07×1.3 **g** 0.0051×0.23 **k** 7.31×1.2

   d 0.11×0.45 **h** 27×1.3 **l** 1430×23

5 A can of Fizzicola contains 0.3 litres of drink. A box holds 36 cans. How many litres of Fizzicola are there in a box?

6 Here are two multiplagons. On each straight line, the numbers in the circles multiply together to make the number in the rectangle. Your job is to copy and complete the multiplagons by filling in the missing numbers.

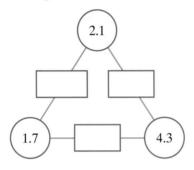
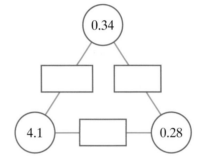

7 Get Real!

Rachel is making some curtains. She buys 4.2 metres of fabric. The fabric costs £3.80 per metre.

  a How much does Rachel have to pay?

  b The fabric is 1.2 metres wide. What area of fabric has Rachel bought?

8 Toby says $0.4 \times 0.2 = 0.8$
Austin says it isn't, because $4 \times 0.2 = 0.8$
Austin says $0.4 \times 0.2 = 0.08$
Toby says it isn't because that's less than you started with.
Who is right, Toby or Austin?
Give a reason for your answer.

9 a You know $3 \times 2 = 6$.
So what is 0.3×0.2?

  b What other multiplications have the same answer as 0.3×0.2?

  c Write down five multiplications with an answer of 0.12

10 a Work out the area of the shape on the right.

  b Estimate the area of the shape to make sure your answer is the right size.

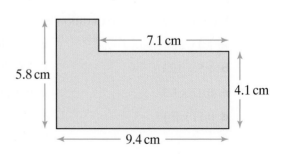

Explore

◎ Add together 1.125 and 9

◎ Now multiply 1.125 by 9

◎ You should get the same answer to both questions

Can you find other pairs of numbers with this characteristic?

Can you find a pair where the product is twice the sum?

$\boxed{\text{Investigate further}}$

Learn 4 Dividing decimals

Examples:

a Calculate $31.2 \div 0.4$

$$31.2 \div 0.4 = \frac{31.2}{0.4}$$

$$= \frac{31.2}{0.4} \xrightarrow{\times 10} = \frac{312}{4}$$ ← Make the fraction an equivalent fraction by multiplying the numerator and denominator by 10

$$\begin{array}{r} 78 \\ 4\overline{\smash{)}312} \end{array}$$ ← Now do the division

So $31.2 \div 0.4 = 78$

b Calculate $3.8 \div 0.05$

$$3.8 \div 0.05 = \frac{3.8}{0.05}$$

$$= \frac{3.8}{0.05} \xrightarrow{\times 10} = \frac{38}{0.5} \xrightarrow{\times 10} = \frac{380}{5}$$ ← Make the fraction an equivalent fraction by multiplying the numerator and denominator by 10 and 10 again

$$\begin{array}{r} 76 \\ 5\overline{\smash{)}380} \end{array}$$ ← Now do the division

So $3.8 \div 0.05 = 76$

Apply 4

1 Write these calculations as equivalent fractions and work them out.

a $3.2 \div 0.4$	**e** $53.1 \div 0.3$	**i** $0.056 \div 0.7$
b $25.4 \div 0.2$	**f** $1.74 \div 0.6$	**j** $1.32 \div 0.004$
c $2.85 \div 0.5$	**g** $0.4 \div 0.08$	**k** $0.028 \div 0.7$
d $42.2 \div 0.02$	**h** $32 \div 0.8$	

2 Write these calculations as equivalent fractions and work them out.

a $4.07 \div 1.1$	**e** $16.8 \div 0.12$	**i** $0.0552 \div 0.012$
b $22.8 \div 1.2$	**f** $25.3 \div 0.11$	**j** $0.945 \div 1.5$
c $2.73 \div 0.13$	**g** $7.392 \div 0.11$	**k** $2.46 \div 0.0015$
d $0.264 \div 1.1$	**h** $0.474 \div 0.12$	**l** $56.2 \div 0.25$

3 Get Real!

Malcolm the plumber has a 6 metre length of copper pipe.
He needs to cut it into 0.4 metre lengths.
How many pieces will he get?

4 Get Real!

On her birthday, Bridget is given a big box of small sweets
called Little Diamonds.
She wants to find out how many sweets are in the box, but it
would take too long to count them.
A label on the box tells her that the total weight is 500 g.
She weighs 10 sweets. The weight of the 10 sweets is 0.4 g.

a How much does one sweet weigh?

b How many sweets are there in the box?

5 Hazel says that $48 \div 2 = 24$, so $48 \div 0.2 = 2.4$
Darren says $48 \div 2 = 24$, so $4.8 \div 0.2 = 2.4$
Harry says $48 \div 2 = 24$, so $4.8 \div 2 = 2.4$
Who is right? Give a reason for your answer.

6 €1 is worth £0.60. How many euro would you get for £7.50?

7 Here are two multiplagons.
On each straight line, the numbers in the circles multiply together
to make the number in the rectangle.
Your job is to copy and complete them by filling in the missing numbers.

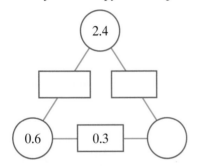

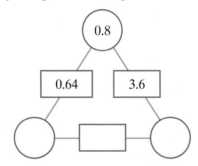

8 Carrie knows that $3.4 \div 0.4 = 8.5$
Use this to copy and fill in the gaps in these questions.

a $34 \div 0.4 = \boxed{}$ **c** $340 \div \boxed{} = 8.5$ **e** $\boxed{} \div 0.04 = 8.5$

b $3.4 \div 4 = \boxed{}$ **d** $\boxed{} \div 4 = 0.85$ **f** $0.34 \div 8.5 = \boxed{}$

9 Start with a number less than 1.   *Example:*   0.8
Take it away from 1. $1 - 0.8$ $= 0.2$
Divide the first number by the second. $0.8 \div 0.2 = 8 \div 2$ $= 4$
Divide this number by one more than itself. $4 \div 5$ $= 0.8$
You end up with the starting number!

Try this yourself, starting with

a 0.5   **b** 0.9   **c** 0.75

Check it with any number you like – although you will probably need a
calculator for more difficult examples.

Explore

- ◎ Draw a grid like this one:

  $\boxed{}$. $\boxed{}$ ÷ $\boxed{0}$. $\boxed{}$

- ◎ Roll a die
- ◎ Write the score in one of the empty boxes in your grid
- ◎ Roll the die twice more, writing the score in a box after each roll
- ◎ Work out the answer to the division
- ◎ Now try again – your aim is to get the highest possible answer

Investigate further

Learn 5 Fractions and decimals

Examples:

a Write 0.72 as a fraction.

To change a decimal to a fraction, just remember the place values.

Units — Tenths — Hundredths

Remember to use the place value of the *last* digit as the denominator

$$0 \,.\, 7 \quad 2 \quad = \frac{72}{100} = \frac{18}{25}$$

The numerator and denominator have been divided by 4

$$0.72 = \frac{18}{25}$$

b Write $\frac{7}{8}$ as a decimal.

$\frac{7}{8}$ means $7 \div 8$.

$$\begin{array}{r} 0\,.\,8\,7\,5 \\ 8\overline{)7\,.\,{}^7 0\,{}^6 0\,{}^4 0} \end{array}$$

You can check your answers with a calculator

$$\frac{7}{8} = 0.875$$

Apply 5

1 Write these decimals as fractions, giving your answers in their simplest form.

a 0.6	**e** 0.65	**i** 0.375
b 0.32	**f** 0.125	**j** 0.015
c 0.9	**g** 0.55	
d 0.8	**h** 0.24	

2 Change these fractions to decimals.

a $\frac{4}{5}$ **b** $\frac{7}{10}$ **c** $\frac{11}{20}$ **d** $\frac{11}{5}$

3 a Write these fractions as decimals.

i $\frac{2}{5}$ **ii** $\frac{3}{8}$ **iii** $\frac{9}{20}$

b Use your answers to part **a** to write the fractions in order of size, starting with the smallest.

4 Which of these fractions is closest to 0.67?

a $\frac{3}{4}$ **b** $\frac{5}{8}$ **c** $\frac{3}{5}$

HINT Write the fractions as decimals.

5 a What is 2.65 as a fraction?

b What is $3\frac{7}{20}$ as a decimal?

6 Josh divided one number by another, and 2.375 was the answer. Both numbers were less than 20. What were the two numbers?

7 Write down five fractions that are equal to 0.4

8 Get Real!

At a school fête, some children decided to raise money with a 'Guess the weight of the cake' stall.
Amy guessed 3300 g, Tariq guessed 3.28 kg and Caroline guessed $3\frac{1}{5}$ kg.
The real weight was 3.237 kg. Who won?

9 Hilary says that $\frac{1}{8} = 1.8$

Nick says $\frac{3}{8} = 0.38$

Eleanor says $\frac{1}{10} = 0.10$

Jeff says $\frac{1}{20} = 0.20$

Who is correct? Correct the errors of the others.

10 Dan knows that $\frac{1}{8} = 0.125$

Use this answer to change these fractions to decimals:

a $\frac{3}{8}$ **b** $1\frac{1}{8}$ **c** $\frac{5}{8}$ **d** $\frac{1}{16}$

11 Write these fractions as decimals. Be careful – they never end!
They are called recurring decimals.
Stop when you have reached a repeating digit or pattern of digits.

a $\frac{2}{3}$ **b** $\frac{4}{11}$ **c** $\frac{3}{7}$

12 Find three fractions that fit all these rules:

a All three fractions must have different denominators.

b Each denominator must be less than 10.

c The fraction must be greater than 0.2

d The fraction must be less than 0.3

Explore

- ◎ Change all the unit fractions ($\frac{1}{2}$, $\frac{1}{3}$, $\frac{1}{4}$, $\frac{1}{5}$, ...) up to $\frac{1}{10}$ to decimals
- ◎ Which give recurring decimals and which give terminating decimals?

(Investigate further)

Decimals

ASSESS

The following exercise tests your understanding of this chapter, with the questions appearing in order of increasing difficulty.

1 Write the numbers below as decimal numbers.

a six tenths

b five hundredths

c eight thousandths

d twelve hundredths

e thirty-five thousandths

f five and nine tenths

g eleven and seven hundredths

h six and one tenth and two thousandths

i one half

j one quarter

k two fifths

l three per cent

2 What is the value of the 5 in the following numbers?

a 325　　b 3526　　c 42.57　　d 3.00543　　e 0.00005

3 Find the 'odd one out' of the following calculations.

a 3.26 + 4.76 + 2.23
　2.76 + 5.13 + 2.46
　4.61 + 3.79 + 1.85

b 7.63 + 6.87 − 5.55
　4.68 + 7.59 − 3.31
　5.23 + 6.41 − 2.68

c 14.22 − 18.46 + 12.67
　12.64 − 14.86 + 9.65
　15.72 + 10.54 − 18.83

4 a Jack and Jill fell down the hill. Jack fell 8.25 m and Jill fell 3.075 m further than Jack.
How far did Jill fall altogether?

b Captain Birdsi took his yacht on a 15.5 km race. The first leg of the race was 3.876 km and the second leg was 6.407 km. How long was the final leg of the race?

c Millie's puppy, Thomas, takes her for walks. On Sunday they walked 5.07 km; on Monday they walked 3.34 km; on Tuesday they walked 4.02 km; on Wednesday they walked 2.29 km; on Thursday they walked 4.8 km; on Friday they walked 2.67 km.
If Millie and Thomas walked a total of 26 km during the week, how far did they walk on Saturday?

d Tony wants to make the picture frame shown below.

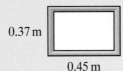

0.37 m

0.45 m

He has a suitable piece of wood one and a half metres long. Is there enough wood to make the frame? Depending on your answer, how much is either left over or needed?

e Delia is making cakes. She uses 0.135 kg sultanas in the first cake, 0.27 kg in the second, 0.185 kg in the third and 0.125 kg in the fourth. How many kilograms of sultanas does she have left from a 1 kg bag?

5 Work out the following:

a 0.4×0.7 **c** 0.02×0.235 **e** 4.025×12.5

b 2.1×11 **d** 20.4×4.3

f Mr Burton, the tailor, is cutting cloth for suits. Each suit takes 4.6 m of cloth. How much cloth is needed for 14 suits?

g One kilogram of nectarines costs £2.95. How much do 15 kilograms cost?

h Jane weighed 2.9 kg when she was born. On her first birthday she was 5.2 times as heavy. How heavy was she on her first birthday? Give your answer to the nearest 100 grams.

i A supermarket stocks boxes of the new breakfast cereal 'Chocobix'. Each packet of 'Chocobix' holds 625 g inside a cardboard box weighing 63 g. The supermarket shelf holds 36 of these packets. What is the total mass, in kilograms, on the shelf?

6 a Convert the following fractions to decimals:
  i $\frac{3}{4}$ **ii** $\frac{1}{8}$ **iii** $\frac{4}{5}$ **iv** $\frac{7}{16}$ **v** $\frac{14}{25}$

b Convert the following decimals to fractions:
  i 0.25   **ii** 0.375   **iii** 0.45   **iv** 0.16   **v** 0.6875

7 a Work out the following:
  i $1.68 \div 0.4$ **iii** $16.9 \div 1.3$ **v** $49.2 \div 1.2$
  ii $220 \div 0.05$ **iv** $6.25 \div 0.25$

b Road Runner travels 3.64 m in 0.7 seconds. How fast is this in metres per second?

c Naomi sees 54 suspect cells under her microscope in an area 0.06 cm². How many cells would she expect to find in an area of 1 cm²?

d A bag of sweets weighing 95 g includes wrappings of 0.5 g. Each sweet weighs 4.5 g. How many sweets are in the bag?

4 Fractions

OBJECTIVES

G   **Examiners would normally expect students who get a G grade to be able to:**

Find equivalent fractions

F   **Examiners would normally expect students who get an F grade also to be able to:**

Simplify fractions, such as $\frac{24}{36}$

Arrange fractions in order of size

E   **Examiners would normally expect students who get an E grade also to be able to:**

Work out fractions of quantities, such as $\frac{5}{8}$ of £20

Find one number as a fraction of another

Do calculations with simple fractions involving addition and multiplication

Convert fractions such as $\frac{3}{8}$ to decimals

D   **Examiners would normally expect students who get a D grade also to be able to:**

Do calculations with simple fractions involving subtraction

C   **Examiners would normally expect students who get a C grade also to be able to:**

Do calculations with simple fractions involving division

Do calculations with mixed numbers

What you should already know ...

■ Understand basic fractions

■ Understand numerator and denominator

39

Fraction or **simple fraction** or **common fraction** or **vulgar fraction** – a number written as one whole number over another, for example, $\frac{3}{8}$ (three eighths), which has the same value as $3 \div 8$

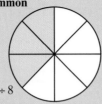

Numerator – the top number in a fraction

Numerator $\longrightarrow \dfrac{3}{8} \longleftarrow$ Denominator

Denominator – the bottom number in a fraction

Unit fraction – a fraction with a numerator of 1, for example, $\frac{1}{5}$

Proper fraction – a fraction in which the numerator is smaller than the denominator, for example, $\frac{5}{13}$

Improper fraction or **top-heavy fraction** – a fraction in which the numerator is bigger than the denominator, for example, $\frac{13}{5}$, which is equal to the mixed number $2\frac{3}{5}$

Mixed number or **mixed fraction** – a number made up of a whole number and a fraction, for example, $2\frac{3}{5}$, which is equal to the improper fraction $\frac{13}{5}$

Decimal fraction – a fraction consisting of tenths, hundredths, thousandths, and so on, expressed in a decimal form, for example, 0.65 (6 tenths and 5 hundredths)

Equivalent fraction – a fraction that has the same value as another, for example, $\frac{3}{5}$ is equivalent to $\frac{30}{50}, \frac{6}{10}, \frac{60}{100}, \frac{15}{25}, \frac{1.5}{2.5}, \dots$

Simplify a fraction or **express a fraction in its simplest form** – to change a fraction to the simplest equivalent fraction; to do this divide the numerator and the denominator by a common factor (this process is called cancelling or reducing or simplifying the fraction)

Learn 1 Equivalent fractions

Example:

Write down a fraction equivalent to $\frac{9}{12}$

This diagram shows a number line from 0 to 1 split up into twelfths and into quarters.

$\frac{1}{12}$	$\frac{2}{12}$	$\frac{3}{12}$	$\frac{4}{12}$	$\frac{5}{12}$	$\frac{6}{12}$	$\frac{7}{12}$	$\frac{8}{12}$	$\frac{9}{12}$	$\frac{10}{12}$	$\frac{11}{12}$	$\frac{12}{12}$
$\frac{1}{4}$			$\frac{2}{4}$			$\frac{3}{4}$			$\frac{4}{4}$		

The shading shows that nine twelfths is the same as three quarters, $\frac{9}{12} = \frac{3}{4}$

In other words, $\frac{9}{12}$ and $\frac{3}{4}$ are equivalent fractions.

The fractions can be changed into one another: $\dfrac{9}{12} \overset{\div 3}{\underset{\div 3}{=}} \dfrac{3}{4}$ and $\dfrac{3}{4} \overset{\times 3}{\underset{\times 3}{=}} \dfrac{9}{12}$

The value of a fraction does not change if you multiply the top number (numerator) and the bottom number (denominator) by the same number.

The value of a fraction does not change if you divide the numerator and the denominator by the same number.

Apply 1

You should be able to do all these questions without a calculator, but you may want to use a calculator to check your work and to speed things up. Find out how to use the $a^{b/c}$ key if you have one on your calculator.

1 Copy and complete these equivalent fraction statements.

a $\dfrac{5}{6} = \dfrac{\square}{12}$

b $\dfrac{3}{12} = \dfrac{\square}{4}$

c $\dfrac{6}{12} = \dfrac{\square}{4} = \dfrac{1}{2}$

d $\dfrac{12}{12} = \dfrac{4}{\square} = 1$

2

$\frac{1}{10}$	$\frac{2}{10}$	$\frac{3}{10}$	$\frac{4}{10}$	$\frac{5}{10}$	$\frac{6}{10}$	$\frac{7}{10}$	$\frac{8}{10}$	$\frac{9}{10}$	$\frac{10}{10}$
$\frac{1}{5}$		$\frac{2}{5}$		$\frac{3}{5}$		$\frac{4}{5}$		$\frac{5}{5}$	
$\frac{1}{2}$					$\frac{2}{2}$				

Use this diagram to copy and complete these equivalent fraction statements.

a $\dfrac{3}{5} = \dfrac{6}{\square}$

b $\dfrac{\square}{\square} = \dfrac{1}{2}$

c $\dfrac{\square}{10} = \dfrac{\square}{5} = \dfrac{\square}{2} = 1$

d Use the diagram to write down another statement about equivalent fractions.

3 Use this circle diagram to write some equivalent fraction statements.

Each part is one twelfth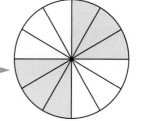

4 Copy and complete these equivalent fraction statements.
Use diagrams to help you if you need to.

a $\dfrac{3}{4} = \dfrac{\square}{8}$

b $\dfrac{2}{\square} = \dfrac{1}{4}$

c $\dfrac{1}{\square} = \dfrac{2}{\square} = \dfrac{4}{8}$

d $\dfrac{8}{\square} = \dfrac{4}{\square} = \dfrac{2}{\square} = 1$

e $\dfrac{1}{3} = \dfrac{\square}{6} = \dfrac{\square}{9} = \dfrac{\square}{12} = \dfrac{\square}{15}$

5 Jack says that $\frac{3}{5} = \frac{6}{8}$

Is he correct? Explain your answer.

6 Mark says 'If the numerator and the denominator of a fraction are the same, the fraction is equal to 1.'
Is Mark correct? Explain your answer.

7 Write down five fractions that are equivalent to $\frac{2}{3}$

8 Find the odd fraction out in this list: $\frac{8}{10}, \frac{6}{8}, \frac{4}{5}, \frac{16}{20}$

Now do the question by changing each of the fractions to decimal form.

9 Write the simplest possible equivalent fraction for each of these fractions.

(Make sure that you know how to do these without a calculator but also find out how to use a calculator to help you simplify fractions.
The simplest way is to use the $\boxed{a^{b/c}}$ key if you have one.)

a $\dfrac{8}{16}$ **f** $\dfrac{18}{36}$ **k** $\dfrac{37}{74}$ **p** $\dfrac{30}{300}$

b $\dfrac{20}{30}$ **g** $\dfrac{12}{16}$ **l** $\dfrac{72}{120}$ **q** $\dfrac{100}{75}$

c $\dfrac{15}{20}$ **h** $\dfrac{15}{24}$ **m** $\dfrac{15}{150}$

d $\dfrac{24}{36}$ **i** $\dfrac{30}{72}$ **n** $\dfrac{2.5}{3.5}$

e $\dfrac{75}{100}$ **j** $\dfrac{45}{100}$ **o** $\dfrac{\frac{1}{2}}{\frac{3}{2}}$

This is a 'top-heavy' (improper) fraction but it can still be simplified

10 Write down three equivalent fraction statements about fifths, tenths and twentieths.

11 Write down an equivalent fraction statement about hundredths, tenths and fifths.

12 Get Real!

A bar of chocolate is spilt into 24 equal pieces and Sam eats 4 of them.

Joe has another bar of chocolate the same size that is split into 30 equal pieces.

How many pieces of that bar should Joe eat so that he eats the same amount of chocolate as Sam?

Explore

Fractions can be marked on a grid like this one. The dot shows $\frac{1}{4}$, because its numerator is 1 and its denominator is 4.

◎ Make a grid like this, going up to 12 in each direction

◎ Mark all the fractions that are equivalent to 1 ($\frac{1}{1}, \frac{2}{2}, \frac{3}{3}$, etc.) What do you notice?

◎ Mark two more sets of equivalent fractions
Compare one set with the other
What is the same and what is different?

◎ Where do top-heavy (improper) fractions appear on the grid?

◎ How can this grid help you to arrange fractions in order?

◎ How can the grid help you to simplify fractions?

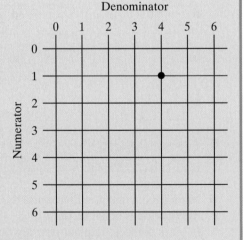

Investigate further

Learn 2 Arranging fractions

Example:

Arrange the following fractions in order of size, largest first.

$$\frac{2}{3}, \frac{1}{4}, \frac{5}{6}, \frac{1}{12}, \frac{1}{2}$$

In order to put fractions in order of size, first change them all to the same denominator.

$$\frac{2}{3}, \frac{1}{4}, \frac{5}{6}, \frac{1}{12}, \frac{1}{2}$$

All the denominators are factors of 12, so all the fractions can be converted to twelfths

Change the fractions to twelfths: $\frac{2}{3} \overset{\times 4}{\underset{\times 4}{=}} \frac{8}{12}$ and so on.

So the list $\frac{2}{3}, \frac{1}{4}, \frac{5}{6}, \frac{1}{12}, \frac{1}{2}$ becomes $\frac{8}{12}, \frac{3}{12}, \frac{10}{12}, \frac{1}{12}, \frac{6}{12}$

which in order of size is $\frac{1}{12}, \frac{3}{12}, \frac{6}{12}, \frac{8}{12}, \frac{10}{12}$

Apply 2

All these questions can be done without a calculator and you should make sure that you are able to do without. Also make sure that you can use your calculator to speed up and to check your work, using your $\boxed{a^{b/c}}$ *key if you have one.*

1 Change these fractions to fifteenths and then arrange them in order of size.

$$\frac{7}{15}, \frac{2}{5}, \frac{2}{3}, \frac{4}{15}$$

2 Change these fractions to hundredths and then arrange them in order of size.

$$\frac{7}{10}, \frac{2}{5}, \frac{27}{50}, \frac{16}{25}$$

Fractions with a denominator of 100 are percentages, for example, $\frac{70}{100}$ is 70%

3 Arrange these fractions in order of size: $\frac{2}{3}, \frac{2}{5}, \frac{1}{2}, \frac{7}{10}$

4 a What is a good common denominator for arranging halves, eighths and quarters in order?

 b Explain why it is not easy to change fifths to twelfths.

5 a Carlo says 'Four fifths is smaller than four sevenths.' Is he correct?

 b Jack says 'Eight ninths is smaller than nine tenths.' Is he correct?

6 a Find three fractions that are bigger than one quarter and smaller than one half.

 b Find a fraction between nine tenths and one.

Explore

◎ Choose any simple fraction, for example $\frac{3}{4}$

◎ Add one to the numerator and one to the denominator, for example $\frac{3+1}{4+1} = \frac{4}{5}$

◎ Find out whether the new fraction is less than, bigger than or the same size as the original fraction

Investigate further

Learn 3 Fractions of quantities

Example:

There are 54 people in a choir. Two thirds of the choir are women. How many women are there in the choir?

To find the number of women in the choir you need to find $\frac{2}{3}$ of 54.

To work out two thirds of 54, first work out one third of 54, then multiply the answer by two to find two thirds.

$\frac{1}{3}$ of 54 = 54 ÷ 3 = 18   ◄——— $\frac{1}{3}$ of 54 ———►

So

| 18 | 36 | 54 |

$\frac{2}{3}$ of 54 = 18 × 2 = 36   ◄——— $\frac{2}{3}$ of 54 ———►

There are 36 women in the choir.

It doesn't matter whether you divide by three and then multiply by two or multiply by two and then divide by three – the result is the same.

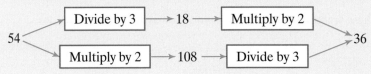

Apply 3

1 Work out:

a $\frac{2}{3}$ of 12

b $\frac{2}{3}$ of £15

c $\frac{2}{3}$ of £30

d $\frac{2}{3}$ × £18

e $150 \times \frac{2}{3}$

f $\frac{2}{3}$ of an hour (find the answer in minutes)

2 Explain how you can use the answer to question **1b** to find the answer to question **1c**.

3 a Two thirds of a number is 10. What is the number?

b Two thirds of a number is 20. What is the number?

4 Find three quarters of:

   a 100

   b 50

   c an hour (answer in minutes)

   d a metre (answer in centimetres)

   e a kilogram (answer in grams)

5 Three quarters of a number is 15. What is the number?

6 Find $\frac{4}{3}$ of:

   a £15   **b** £30   **c** £18   **d** 150   **e** an hour

7 Which of these calculations will work out $\frac{3}{5}$ of 44?
Write down all of the calculations that apply.

   a $44 \div 5 \times 3$ **c** $44 \times 5 \div 3$ **e** $44 \div 100 \times 60$

   b $44 \div 3 \times 5$ **d** $44 \times 3 \div 5$ **f** $44 \times 10 \div 6$

8 Get Real!

A type of bronze used to make coins is made up of copper, tin and zinc.

$\frac{95}{100}$ of the bronze is copper, $\frac{4}{100}$ is tin and the rest is zinc.

How much tin is there in 2 kg of bronze?

Explore

  ◎ Find $\frac{3}{4}$ of 20

  ◎ Now find $\frac{4}{3}$ of the result

  ◎ What do you notice?

  ◎ Can you explain what has happened?

Investigate further

Learn 4 One quantity as a fraction of another

A total of 28 students took a maths test and 16 students passed the test.
What fraction of the students passed the test?

This is the number of ⟶ $\frac{16}{28}$ ⟵ This is the number of
students who took the test   students who passed the test

The fraction $\frac{16}{28}$ can be simplified to $\frac{4}{7}$.   Reminder: $\frac{16}{28} = \frac{4}{7}$ (÷4 ÷4)

So $\frac{4}{7}$ of the class passed the test and   These results could also be expressed
$\frac{3}{7}$ of the class did not pass it.   as decimals or percentages

In everyday life, percentages are usually used

Apply 4

You should be able to do all these without a calculator.
You may like to use your calculator to check your answers.

1   If there are 28 students in the class, what fraction of them passed the test if the number passing was:

   a 14   **b** 12   **c** 13   **d** 18   **e** 20?

   f If the fraction passing the test was $\frac{3}{4}$, how many students passed?

   g Explain why you should never get an improper (top-heavy) fraction in a question like this.

2   Here is a list of the test marks of a class of 30 students, arranged in order.

     22   25
     30   33   37
     42   43   46   46
     53   54   55   55   56
     61   61   63   64   64   67   68   68   69
     73   75   78   79
     81   87
     95

   a What fraction of the students got under 40 marks?

   b What fraction of the students got a mark in the sixties?

   c If the pass mark was 50 marks what fraction of the students would pass the test?

   d What should the pass mark be for two thirds of the students to pass the test?

   e What mark separates the top tenth of the class from the rest?

3 Get Real!

A T-shirt costing £7.50 has its price reduced by £1.50 in a sale.

a What fraction reduction is this?

b What fraction of the original price is the sale price?

c If the price of the T-shirt was reduced by $\frac{1}{3}$ what would the sale price be?

d If the sale price of a T-shirt was £6 after a reduction of $\frac{1}{3}$, what was the original price?

£7.50

4 This graph shows the price of petrol in different countries.
The wholesale price and the taxes make up the price at the pump.

a Estimate what fraction of its total petrol price each country pays in tax.

b Which country pays the highest fraction in tax?

c Which country pays the lowest fraction in tax?

d The prices are given in US dollars. Would it affect your answers if the prices were given in euro? Explain your answer.

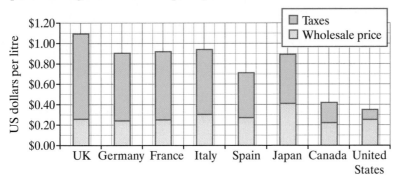

Explore

◎ In this diagram, what fraction of the outside square is black?

◎ What fraction is white?

◎ Now another black square has been added

◎ What fraction of the outside square is the new black square?

◎ What fraction of the outside square is black now?

◎ What fraction is white?

◎ Now another white square has been added

◎ What fraction of the outside square is the new white square?

◎ What fraction of the outside square is black now?

◎ What fraction is white?

Investigate further

Learn 5 Adding and subtracting fractions

Examples:

a Calculate $\frac{5}{6} + \frac{3}{4}$

Fractions cannot be added (or subtracted) unless they have the same denominator.

$\frac{5}{6} + \frac{3}{4}$ ←———— Change both the fractions to twelfths

$= \frac{10}{12} + \frac{9}{12}$ ←———— When the fractions have both been changed to

$= \frac{19}{12}$ ←———— twelfths, add to find the total number of twelfths

$= 1\frac{7}{12}$ ←———— Simplify the answer by writing it as a mixed number

Reminder: $\dfrac{5}{6} \overset{\times 2}{\underset{\times 2}{=}} \dfrac{10}{12}$ and $\dfrac{3}{4} \overset{\times 3}{\underset{\times 3}{=}} \dfrac{9}{12}$

b Calculate $\frac{5}{6} - \frac{3}{4}$

$\frac{5}{6} - \frac{3}{4}$

$= \frac{10}{12} - \frac{9}{12}$

$= \frac{1}{12}$

c Calculate $1\frac{5}{6} + 2\frac{3}{4}$

$1\frac{5}{6} + 2\frac{3}{4}$

$= 1 + \frac{5}{6} + 2 + \frac{3}{4}$

$= 3 + \frac{10}{12} + \frac{9}{12}$

$= 3\frac{19}{12} = 4\frac{7}{12}$

d Calculate $2\frac{1}{6} - \frac{3}{4}$

$2\frac{1}{6} - \frac{3}{4}$

$= 2 + \frac{2}{12} - \frac{9}{12}$

$= 2 - \frac{7}{12}$ ←———— Change one of the units to twelfths to do this subtraction

$= 1\frac{5}{12}$ $2 - \frac{7}{12} = 1 + 1 - \frac{7}{12} = 1 + \frac{12}{12} - \frac{7}{12} = 1\frac{5}{12}$

Apply 5

Questions like this will be on the non-calculator paper so make sure you can do them without using your calculator.

1 Work out: **a** $\frac{3}{4} + \frac{2}{3}$ **b** $\frac{3}{4} - \frac{2}{3}$ **c** $\frac{5}{6} + \frac{2}{5}$ **d** $\frac{5}{6} - \frac{2}{5}$

2 Work out: **a** $3\frac{3}{4} + 1\frac{2}{3}$ **b** $3\frac{3}{4} - 1\frac{2}{3}$ **c** $2\frac{5}{6} + 1\frac{2}{5}$ **d** $2\frac{5}{6} - 1\frac{2}{5}$

3 Work out: **a** $3\frac{2}{3} + 1\frac{3}{4}$ **b** $3\frac{2}{3} - 1\frac{3}{4}$ **c** $2\frac{2}{5} + 1\frac{5}{6}$ **d** $2\frac{2}{5} - 1\frac{5}{6}$

4 Sue says 'I add up fractions like this: $\frac{5}{6} + \frac{2}{5} = \frac{5+2}{6+5} = \frac{7}{11}$,'
Is Sue right? Explain your answer.

5 Find two fractions with:

a a sum of $1\frac{1}{4}$

b a difference of $1\frac{1}{4}$

c a sum of $3\frac{1}{3}$

d a difference of $3\frac{1}{3}$

6 Get Real!

Anne is making custard, which needs $\frac{1}{3}$ of a cup of sugar.

Then she makes biscuits, which need $\frac{3}{4}$ of a cup of sugar.

Anne only has 1 cup of sugar.
Does she have enough to make the custard and the biscuits?
Show how you got your answer.

7 Get Real!

In America, lengths of fabric for making clothes are measured in yards and fractions of yards.
A tailor is making a suit for a customer.
The jacket needs $2\frac{1}{4}$ yards of fabric and the trousers need $1\frac{1}{3}$ yards.
The tailor has 4 yards of fabric.
How much will be left over when he has made the jacket and the trousers?

Explore

A man was riding a camel across a desert, when he came across three young men arguing. Their father had died, leaving seventeen camels as his sons' inheritance. The eldest son was to receive half of the camels; the second son, one-third of the camels and the youngest son, one-ninth of the camels. The sons asked him how they could divide seventeen camels in this way.

The man added his camel to the 17. Then, he gave $\frac{1}{2}$ of the camels to the eldest son, $\frac{1}{3}$ of the camels to the second son and $\frac{1}{9}$ of the camels to the youngest son. Having solved the problem, the stranger mounted his own camel and rode away.

How does this work?

Investigate further

Learn 6 Multiplying and dividing fractions

Examples:

a Calculate:

   i $12 \times \frac{1}{3}$ **ii** $12 \times \frac{2}{3}$ **iii** $\frac{3}{4} \times \frac{2}{3}$

   i $12 \times \frac{1}{3}$ ◄——— Multiplying by $\frac{1}{3}$ is the same as dividing by 3

     $= \frac{12}{3}$

     $= 4$

   ii $12 \times \frac{2}{3}$ ◄——— Multiplying by $\frac{2}{3}$ is the same as dividing by 3 and multiplying by 2

     $= \frac{24}{3}$

     $= 8$

   iii $\frac{3}{4} \times \frac{2}{3}$

     $= \frac{3 \times 2}{4 \times 3}$

     $= \frac{6}{12}$

     $= \frac{1}{2}$

b Calculate:

   i $8 \div \frac{1}{3}$ **ii** $8 \div \frac{2}{3}$ **iii** $\frac{3}{4} \div \frac{2}{3}$

   i $8 \div \frac{1}{3}$ ◄——— Dividing 8 by a third means finding how many thirds there are in 8
                                 There are three thirds in each whole, so there

     $= 8 \times \frac{3}{1}$ are 8×3 thirds in 8

     $= 24$

   ii $8 \div \frac{2}{3}$ ◄——— The number of two-thirds in 8 is half the number of thirds in 8

     $= 8 \times \frac{3}{2}$ Dividing by $\frac{2}{3}$ is the same as multiplying by $\frac{3}{2}$

     $= 12$

   iii $\frac{3}{4} \div \frac{2}{3}$

     $= \frac{3}{4} \times \frac{3}{2}$ ◄——— Dividing by a fraction is the same as multiplying by the reciprocal (upside-down) fraction

     $= \frac{3 \times 3}{4 \times 2}$

     $= \frac{9}{8}$

     $= 1\frac{1}{8}$

Apply 6

1 Work out:

   a $18 \times \frac{1}{3}$ **c** $35 \times \frac{1}{7}$ **e** $40 \times \frac{2}{5}$ **g** $24 \times \frac{5}{8}$

   b $28 \times \frac{1}{4}$ **d** $40 \times \frac{1}{5}$ **f** $12 \times \frac{3}{4}$ **h** $42 \times \frac{5}{6}$

2 Work out:

   a $\frac{4}{5} \times \frac{1}{2}$ **c** $\frac{5}{6} \times \frac{1}{4}$ **e** $\frac{5}{8} \times \frac{3}{5}$ **g** $\frac{11}{12} \times \frac{4}{5}$

   b $\frac{3}{8} \times \frac{1}{3}$ **d** $\frac{9}{10} \times \frac{1}{6}$ **f** $\frac{8}{9} \times \frac{3}{4}$ **h** $\frac{9}{10} \times \frac{2}{3}$

3 Work out:

   a $18 \div \frac{1}{3}$ **c** $6 \div \frac{1}{5}$ **e** $18 \div \frac{2}{3}$ **g** $28 \div \frac{4}{5}$

   b $5 \div \frac{1}{4}$ **d** $10 \div \frac{1}{8}$ **f** $12 \div \frac{3}{4}$ **h** $35 \div \frac{5}{6}$

4 Work out:

   a $\frac{7}{8} \div \frac{1}{2}$ **c** $\frac{4}{9} \div \frac{2}{5}$ **e** $\frac{1}{3} \div \frac{1}{3}$ **g** $\frac{3}{5} \div \frac{7}{10}$

   b $\frac{1}{6} \div \frac{2}{3}$ **d** $\frac{2}{7} \div \frac{2}{3}$ **f** $\frac{1}{3} \div \frac{1}{5}$ **h** $\frac{11}{12} \div \frac{3}{4}$

5 Paula is working out $\frac{4}{15} \div \frac{3}{8}$

   She says, 'I can cancel the 4 into the 8 and the 3 into the 15.'

   Then she writes down $\frac{1}{5} \div \frac{1}{2} = \frac{1}{5} \times \frac{2}{1} = \frac{2}{5}$

   Is this correct? Explain your answer.

6 Ali says, 'This is how to divide fractions: $\frac{5}{6} \div \frac{2}{5} = \frac{6}{5} \times \frac{2}{5} = \frac{12}{25}$,'

   Is Ali right? Explain your answer.

<u>7</u> Without working out the answers, say which of these gives an answer greater than 1:

   $\frac{9}{10} \times \frac{4}{5}$ or $\frac{9}{10} \div \frac{4}{5}$?

   Give a reason for your answer.

8 Write down two fractions that:

   a multiply to give 1   **b** divide to give 1.

9 Get Real!

Two thirds of the teachers in a school are women and three quarters of these are over 40. What fraction of the teachers in the school are women over 40?

10 Get Real!

Seven eighths of the members of the running club train on Wednesday evening and four fifths of them are male. What fraction of the members are males who train on Wednesday evenings?

Fractions

The following exercise tests your understanding of this chapter, with the questions appearing in order of increasing difficulty.

1 a Find the fraction that is shaded in each of the following diagrams. Write each fraction in its simplest form.

i

ii

iii

iv

v

b Copy the following fractions and fill in the gaps.

i $\dfrac{3}{5} = \dfrac{\square}{10}$

ii $\dfrac{3}{4} = \dfrac{\square}{8}$

iii $\dfrac{14}{24} = \dfrac{7}{\square}$

iv $\dfrac{10}{12} = \dfrac{5}{\square}$

v $\dfrac{\square}{24} = \dfrac{5}{8}$

vi $\dfrac{\square}{12} = \dfrac{21}{36}$

vii $\dfrac{9}{\square} = \dfrac{45}{100}$

viii $\dfrac{8}{\square} = \dfrac{32}{60}$

2 a Change these fractions to sixteenths and then put them in order of size, starting with the smallest.

$\dfrac{3}{8}$ $\dfrac{1}{4}$ $\dfrac{7}{8}$ $\dfrac{9}{16}$

b Arrange these fractions in order of size, smallest first.

$\dfrac{2}{3}$ $\dfrac{5}{8}$ $\dfrac{7}{12}$ $\dfrac{11}{24}$

c Which is smaller, $\dfrac{2}{5}$ or $\dfrac{3}{8}$?

3 a Paula is running a 10 000 m race.
How far has she run when she has covered $\frac{5}{8}$ of it?

 b Sunita spent $2\frac{1}{2}$ hours on her homework.
She spent $\frac{2}{5}$ of the time on her maths.
How long did she spend on maths?

 c A bag contains 40 litres of plant food.
Dev uses $\frac{5}{8}$ of it in his patio tubs.
How many litres of plant food does he use?

 d Mr Graham's school has 300 students.
$\frac{4}{15}$ of the students play musical instruments.
How many students play instruments?

 e In a sale the price of a coat, originally £84, was reduced by $\frac{1}{3}$
What is the sale price of the coat?

 4 a Mrs Snow travelled 480 miles to Scotland.
360 miles were on motorways.
What fraction of her journey was on motorways?

 b A Virgin Voyager arrived at Euston station 30 minutes late.
What fraction is this of the timetabled journey time of $2\frac{1}{2}$ hours?

 c What fraction of the word MISSISSIPPI is made up by I's?

 d Old Macdonald had a farm.
He had 18 pigs, 5 goats, 128 sheep, 6 horses,
22 chickens, 20 cows and 1 bull.
What fraction of his livestock are sheep?

 e In an examination sat by 240 students only 100 answered
a particular question correctly.
What fraction got the question wrong?

5 a Ann eats three quarters of a pound of fruit each day.
How much fruit does she eat in seven days?

 b Tony eats $\frac{1}{4}$ kg of fruit each day.
He has 3 kg of fruit.
How many days will it take him to eat his fruit?

6 a Scrooge collects money.

 $\frac{3}{10}$ of his fortune is in bronze coins, $\frac{8}{15}$ is in silver and the rest is in notes.

 What fraction of Scrooge's fortune is in notes?

 b In the 4 × 100 m relay, the first runner took $\frac{1}{5}$ of his team's total time.
The second runner took $\frac{7}{30}$ of their total time.
The third runner took $\frac{3}{10}$ of their total time.

 i What fraction of their time was taken by the fourth member of
the team?

 ii Which team member ran the fastest leg of the race?

 iii Which team member ran the slowest leg of the race?

c Delia is cooking.
She has a $1\frac{1}{2}$ kg bag of flour and needs $\frac{3}{8}$ of it in a recipe.
What fraction of a kilogram does she need and what is this in grams?

d S. Crumpy has an orchard.
The orchard contains $4\frac{1}{3}$ hectares of apple trees.
Today he needs to treat $\frac{4}{5}$ of the area for disease prevention.
What area does he need to treat?

e In a football match the goalkeeper kicked the ball from the goal line for $\frac{5}{8}$ of the length of the pitch and a player then kicked it a further $\frac{5}{24}$
The length of the pitch is 90 yards.
How far is the ball from the opposing goal line?

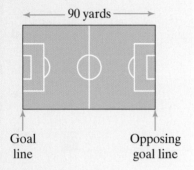

7 a Work out the following:

i $6\frac{3}{7} + 3\frac{6}{7}$ **iii** $9\frac{4}{5} + 6\frac{3}{8}$ **v** $11\frac{2}{7} - 6\frac{4}{5}$ **vii** $10 \div \frac{2}{3}$

ii $8\frac{1}{4} - 4\frac{5}{8}$ **iv** $7\frac{5}{8} - 3\frac{1}{4}$ **vi** $\frac{2}{3} \times \frac{5}{6}$ **viii** $3\frac{1}{5} \div 1\frac{3}{5}$

b i Titus Lines, the fisherman, catches one fish of mass $2\frac{1}{3}$ kg and another of mass $3\frac{1}{4}$ kg. What total mass of fish does he catch?

ii What is the perimeter of a triangle of sides $2\frac{1}{4}$, $3\frac{1}{5}$ and $4\frac{3}{10}$ inches?

iii A can holds $2\frac{8}{9}$ litres of oil. Hakim uses $1\frac{4}{15}$ litres. How much is left?

iv Deirdre drops Ken off at work after driving from home for $4\frac{5}{12}$ miles.
She drives $7\frac{1}{4}$ miles altogether to her own place of work.
How far is Ken's workplace from Deirdre's workplace?

v Milo is $1\frac{2}{7}$ metres tall. He is $\frac{3}{8}$ metre taller than Fizz. How tall is Fizz?

Indices

OBJECTIVES

F **Examiners would normally expect students who get an F grade to be able to:**

Calculate squares and square roots (with and without the use of a calculator)

E **Examiners would normally expect students who get an E grade also to be able to:**

Calculate cubes and cube roots (with and without the use of a calculator)

Use function keys on a calculator for powers and roots

D **Examiners would normally expect students who get a D grade also to be able to:**

Use the terms square, positive square root, negative square root, cube and cube root

Recall integer squares from 2×2 to 15×15 and the corresponding square roots

Recall the cubes of 2, 3, 4, 5 and 10

C **Examiners would normally expect students who get a C grade also to be able to:**

Use index notation and index laws for positive and negative powers such as $w^3 \times w^5$ and $\dfrac{w^3}{w^7}$

What you should already know ...

■ Understand the idea of square numbers

■ Understand the idea of a reciprocals

■ Basic use of algebra

Square number – a square number is the outcome when a number is multiplied by itself

Cube number – a cube number is the outcome when a number is multiplied by itself then multiplied by itself again

Square root – a square root of a number such as 16 is a number whose outcome is 16 when multiplied by itself

Cube root – the cube root of a number such as 125 is a number whose outcome is 125 when multiplied by itself then multiplied by itself again

Index or **power** or **exponent** – the index tells you how many times the base number is to be multiplied by itself

So $5^3 = 5 \times 5 \times 5$

Indices – the plural of index

Learn 1   Powers and roots

Examples: Find: **a** 4^2 **b** 5^3 **c** $\sqrt{16}$ **d** $\sqrt[3]{125}$

a $4^2 = 4 \times 4 = 16$
16 is a square number because $4 \times 4 = 16$.

4 squared -4 squared is $-4 \times -4 = 16$

A square number is a number 'to the power of 2' so 4 squared is also 4 to the power 2 which is written as 4^2.

The square button on a calculator looks like $\boxed{x^2}$

b $5^3 = 5 \times 5 \times 5 = 125$
125 is a cube number because $5 \times 5 \times 5 = 125$.

5 cubed -5 cubed is $-5 \times -5 \times -5 = -125$

A cube number is a number 'to the power of 3' so 5 cubed is also 5 to the power 3 which is written as 5^3.

The cube button on a calculator looks like $\boxed{x^3}$

c $\sqrt{16} = 4$

Four is a square root of 16 as $4 \times 4 = 16$.

The square root of 16 is written as $\sqrt{16}$ or $\sqrt[2]{16}$, so $\sqrt{16} = 4$.

The square root button on a calculator looks like $\boxed{\sqrt{}}$

d $\sqrt[3]{125} = 5$

The cube root of 125 is 5 as $5 \times 5 \times 5 = 125$.

The cube root of 125 is written as $\sqrt[3]{125}$, so $\sqrt[3]{125} = 5$.

The cube root button on a calculator looks like $\boxed{\sqrt[3]{}}$

Apply 1

1 16   27   −7   1   0.2   5   6

From the numbers above, write:

a a square number

c the square root of 49

b a cube number

d the cube root of 1.

2 Write the value of each of these.

a 4^2

e 10^3

i $\sqrt[3]{1}$

b 12^2

f $\sqrt{9}$

j $\sqrt[3]{64}$

c 1.5^2

g $\sqrt{100}$

k $\sqrt[3]{-64}$

d 6^3

h $\sqrt{225}$

3 Calculate these.

a $3^2 + 4^2$

c $10^3 - \sqrt{100}$

e $\sqrt{5^2 + 12^2}$

b $2^3 \times 3^2$

d $\sqrt{225} - \sqrt[3]{125}$

f $\sqrt{3^2 \times 5^2}$

4 Which is larger?

a 2^3 or 3^2

b $\sqrt{64}$ or $\sqrt[3]{125}$

5 Write the value of each of these.

a 2.2^2

e 10.1^3

i $\sqrt[3]{-0.5}$

b 10.1^2

f $\sqrt[3]{1.5}$

j $\sqrt{8}$

c 8.5^2

g $\sqrt{75}$

d 2.2^3

h $\sqrt[3]{0.5}$

6 Neil says -3^2 is 9.
Andrea says -3^2 is −9.
Who is correct?
Give a reason for your answer.

7 Get Real!
A builder is laying a square concrete patio.
The area of the patio is to be 30 cm^2.
Use your calculator to find the length of the sides
correct to one decimal place.

Explore

◎ The number 64 is both a square number and a cube number

◎ Can you find any other numbers that are both square numbers and cube numbers?

(Investigate further)

Explore

◎ Jenny investigates the sum of the cubes of the first two integers
She notices that the sum gives a square number:
$$1^3 + 2^3 = 9 \ (= 3^2)$$

◎ Jenny now investigates the sum of the cubes of the first three integers
She notices, again, that the sum gives a square number:
$$1^3 + 2^3 + 3^3 = 36 \ (= 6^2)$$

◎ Investigate the sum of the cubes of the first four integers

(Investigate further)

Learn 2   Rules of indices

Examples: **a** Work out 5^3.

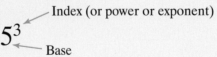

Index (or power or exponent)

5^3

Base

So $5^3 = 5 \times 5 \times 5 = 125$

The index (or power or exponent) tells you how many times the base number is to be multiplied by itself.

You can use the $\boxed{x^y}$ button for indices on your calculator

b Simplify   **i** $a^2 \times a^3$ **ii** $a^3 \times a^5$ **iii** $a^6 \div a^4$ **iv** $a^7 \div a^3$
       v $(a^4)^2$ **vi** $(a^2)^3$

i $a^2 \times a^3 = (a \times a) \times (a \times a \times a)$
$\quad = a \times a \times a \times a \times a$
$\quad = a^5$

ii $a^3 \times a^5 = (a \times a \times a) \times (a \times a \times a \times a \times a)$
$\quad = a \times a \times a \times a \times a \times a \times a \times a$
$\quad = a^8$

So $a^2 \times a^3 = a^5$
and $a^3 \times a^5 = a^8$

You should notice that

$a^2 \times a^3 = a^{2+3} = a^5$
and $a^3 \times a^5 = a^{3+5} = a^8$

iii $a^6 \div a^4 = \dfrac{a^6}{a^4}$

$= \dfrac{a \times a \times a \times a \times a \times a}{a \times a \times a \times a}$

$= \dfrac{\cancel{a}_1 \times \cancel{a}_1 \times \cancel{a}_1 \times \cancel{a}_1 \times a \times a}{\cancel{a}_1 \times \cancel{a}_1 \times \cancel{a}_1 \times \cancel{a}_1}$

$= a \times a$

$= a^2$

iv $a^7 \div a^3 = \dfrac{a^7}{a^3}$

$= \dfrac{a \times a \times a \times a \times a \times a \times a}{a \times a \times a}$

$= \dfrac{\cancel{a}_1 \times \cancel{a}_1 \times \cancel{a}_1 \times a \times a \times a \times a}{\cancel{a}_1 \times \cancel{a}_1 \times \cancel{a}_1}$

$= a \times a \times a \times a$

$= a^4$

So $\qquad a^6 \div a^4 = a^2$

and $\qquad a^7 \div a^3 = a^4$

You should notice that

$\qquad a^6 \div a^4 = a^{6-4} = a^2$

and $\qquad a^7 \div a^3 = a^{7-3} = a^4$

v $(a^4)^2 = a^4 \times a^4$

$= (a \times a \times a \times a) \times (a \times a \times a \times a)$

$= a \times a \times a \times a \times a \times a \times a \times a$

$= a^8$

vi $(a^2)^3 = a^2 \times a^2 \times a^2$

$= (a \times a) \times (a \times a) \times (a \times a)$

$= a \times a \times a \times a \times a \times a$

$= a^6$

So $\qquad (a^4)^2 = a^8$

and $\qquad (a^2)^3 = a^6$

You should notice that

$\qquad (a^4)^2 = a^{4 \times 2} = a^8$

and $\qquad (a^2)^3 = a^{2 \times 3} = a^6$

Apply 2

1 Write the following numbers in index notation.

a $5 \times 5 \times 5 \times 5$

b $2 \times 2 \times 2 \times 2 \times 2 \times 2 \times 2$

c $6 \times 6 \times 6 \times 6 \times 6 \times 6 \times 6 \times 6 \times 6 \times 6 \times 6 \times 6$

d 13×13

e $2 \times 2 \times 2 \times 2 \times 2 \times 2 \times 2 \times 2 \times 2 \times 2 \times 2 \times 2 \times 2 \times 2 \times 2 \times 2 \times 2$

f $12 \times 12 \times 12 \times 12$

g $8 \times 8 \times 8 \times 8 \times 8$

h $1 \times 1 \times 1 \times 1 \times 1 \times 1 \times 1 \times 1 \times 1 \times 1 \times 1 \times 1 \times 1 \times 1 \times 1 \times 1 \times 1 \times 1 \times 1 \times 1$

2 Find the value of each of the following.

a 7^2 **e** 2^3 **i** 3^4 **m** 5^1

b 4^2 **f** 2^4 **j** 4^3 **n** 4^6

c 11^2 **g** 1^5 **k** $(-2)^6$

d $(-3)^2$ **h** 2^5 **l** $(-2)^7$

3 Simplify the following numbers, giving your answers in index form.

a $5^6 \times 5^2$ **e** $4^3 \times 4^8$ **i** $11^{10} \div 11^{14}$ **m** $(6^2)^5$

b $12^8 \times 12^3$ **f** $10^6 \times 10^{12}$ **j** $\dfrac{4^7}{4^3}$ **n** $(11^5)^4$

c $3^5 \div 3^2$ **g** $7^{11} \div 7^6$ **k** $\dfrac{9^{12}}{9^{11}}$ **o** $(10^{10})^{10}$

d $5^6 \times 5^2$ **h** $6^5 \div 6^3$ **l** $\dfrac{25^7}{25^8}$

4 Alison is investigating the rules of indices.
She writes down $4^3 \div 4^3 = 4^{3-3} = 4^0$ $4^3 \div 4^3 = 64 \div 64 = 1$ so $4^0 = 1$
She then writes down $2^5 \div 2^5 = 2^{5-5} = 2^0$ $2^5 \div 2^5 = 32 \div 32 = ...$
$3^4 \div 3^4 = 3^{4-4} = 3^0$ $3^4 \div 3^4 = ...$
$5^2 \div 5^2 = 5^{2-2} = 5^0$ $5^2 \div 5^2 = ...$

Copy and complete Alison's working. What do you notice?
Does this always work?

 5 Find the values of each of the following.

a 2^6 **d** 8^6 **g** $2^6 + 6^2$

b 2^{10} **e** 9^4 **h** $5^5 \times 10^{-4}$

c 3^5 **f** $2^{11} - 5^3$ **i** $10^8 - 10^6$

6 Say whether these statements are true or false? Give a reason for your answer.

a $6^2 = 12$ **c** $\dfrac{2^{10}}{4^5} = 1$ **e** $10^{50} \times 10^{50} = 10^{100}$

b $1^3 = 1$ **d** $3^4 + 3^5 = 3^9$

7 Simplify these leaving your answers in index form.

a $x^6 \times x^2$ **c** $\dfrac{a^7}{a^3}$ **e** $q^7 \div q^{10}$

b $e^8 \times e^3$ **d** $p^{10} \div p^5$ **f** $(b^2)^5$

8 The number 64 can be written in index form as 8^2.
Write down three other ways that 64 can be written in index form.

Explore

◎ Manjula says that 1^n is always 1
   Is Manjula correct?

◎ Try different values of n, for example, positive and negative

Investigate further

Explore

⊚   One grain of rice is placed on the first square of a chessboard

⊚   Two grains of rice are placed on the second square of a chessboard

⊚   Four grains of rice are placed on the third square of a chessboard

⊚   Eight grains of rice are placed on the fourth square of a chessboard etc

How many grains of rice will there be on the fifth square?

How many grains of rice will there be altogether on the first five squares?

How many grains of rice will there be on the tenth square?

How many grains of rice will there be altogether on the first ten squares?

> **Investigate further**

Indices

A S S E S S

The following exercise tests your understanding of this chapter,
with the questions appearing in order of increasing difficulty.

1 Work these out without using a calculator.

   a 4^2 **d** $\sqrt{36}$ **g** 0^2

   b 11^2 **e** $\sqrt{196}$ **h** $(-3)^2$

   c 2.5^2 **f** $\sqrt{1.44}$

2 a Work these out without using a calculator.

   i 5^3 **iii** $\sqrt[3]{27}$ **v** $\sqrt[3]{0}$

   ii 10^3 **iv** $\sqrt[3]{64}$ **vi** $\sqrt[3]{(-8)}$

   b Work these out using the appropriate keys on a calculator.

   i 1.2^3 **iii** $\sqrt[3]{39.304}$ **v** $\sqrt[3]{-10.648}$

   ii 2.5^3 **iv** $\sqrt[3]{166.375}$

3 a Sam says numbers have two square roots.
   George says some numbers have no square roots.
   Who is right? Give a reason for your answer.

   b Amelia joins in the conversation and says that all numbers have two
   cube roots.
   Is she right? Give a reason for your answer.

4 a Work out the following, giving your answers in index form.

    i $4^6 \times 4^2$ **v** $6^4 \times 6^2 \times 6^3$ **ix** $5^8 \div 5^7$

    ii $11^5 \times 11^3$ **vi** $10^4 \div 10^2$ **x** $2^3 \div 2^3$

    iii $(5^3)^2$ **vii** $21^7 \div 21^5$

    iv $7^5 \times 7$ **viii** $16^{10} \div 16^9$

b Find the value of:

    i $3^2 \times 4^2$ **iii** $6^5 \times 6^3 \div 6^4$

    ii $3^4 \div 5^2$ **iv** $\dfrac{(10^8 \times 10^7)}{(10^7 \times 10^6)}$

c Which is larger:

    i 3^5 or 5^3 **ii** 11^2 or 2^{11} **iii** 2^4 or 4^2?

5 Simplify:

    a $x^4 \times x^3$ **c** $z \times z^7$ **e** $q^8 \div q^6$

    b $y^5 \times y^2$ **d** $p^5 \div p^4$ **f** $(t^4)^2$

6 Tom says that $k^4 \div k^6 = k^2$.
Is Tom correct? Explain your answer.

Try a real past exam question to test your knowledge:

7 a Work out the cube of 4.

  b Work out 0.2^2

  c A list of numbers is given below.

    15 16 19 27 34 42 45

  From this list, write:

    i a cube number

    ii a prime number.

Spec B, Int Paper 2, Nov 02

Examiners would normally expect students who get an F grade to be able to:

Understand that percentage means 'out of 100'

Change a percentage to a fraction or a decimal and vice versa

Examiners would normally expect students who get an E grade also to be able to:

Compare percentages, fractions and decimals

Work out a percentage of a given quantity

Calculate simple interest

Examiners would normally expect students who get a D grade also to be able to:

Increase or decrease a quantity by a given percentage

Express one quantity as a percentage of another

Examiners would normally expect students who get a C grade also to be able to:

Work out a percentage increase or decrease

What you should already know ...

- Place values in decimals
  (for example, $0.6 = \frac{6}{10}$, $0.06 = \frac{6}{100}$)

- How to put decimals in order of size

- How to express fractions in their lowest terms (or simplest form)

- How to change a fraction to a decimal and vice versa

Percentage – a number of parts per hundred, for example, 15% means $\frac{15}{100}$

Numerator – the number on the top of a fraction

Numerator $\longrightarrow \dfrac{3}{8} \longleftarrow$ Denominator

Denominator – the number on the bottom of a fraction

Interest – money paid to you by a bank, building society or other financial institution if you put your money in an account or the money you pay for borrowing from a bank

Principal – the money put into the bank or borrowed from the bank

Rate – the percentage at which interest is added, usually expressed as per cent per annum (year)

Time – usually measured in years for the purpose of working out interest

Amount – the total you will have in the bank or the total you will owe the bank, at the end of the period of time

Balance – the amount of money you have in your bank account or the amount of money you owe after you have paid a deposit

Deposit – an amount of money you pay towards the cost of an item, with the rest of the cost to be paid later

Discount – a reduction in the price, perhaps for paying in cash or paying early

VAT (Value Added Tax) – a tax that has to be added on to the price of goods or services

Depreciation – a reduction in value, for example, due to age or condition

Credit – when you buy goods 'on credit' you do not pay all the cost at once; instead you make a number of payments at regular intervals, often once a month

Learn 1   Percentages, fractions and decimals

Examples:

a Convert the following decimals to percentages.

  i 0.76
  ii 0.7

  i 0.76 $= 0.76 \times 100\%$ $= 76\%$ To change a decimal to a percentage,
  ii 0.7 $= 0.7 \times 100\%$ $= 70\%$ multiply by 100 (the digits will move 2 places to the left)

b Convert the following percentages to decimals.

  i 16%
  ii 4%

  i 16% $= 16\% \div 100$ $= 0.16$ To change a percentage to a decimal,
  ii 4% $= 4\% \div 100$ $= 0.04$ divide by 100 (the digits will move 2 places to the right)

c Convert the following fractions to percentages.

  i $\frac{27}{100}$
  ii $\frac{9}{210}$

  i $\frac{27}{100}$ $= \frac{27}{100} \times 100\%$ $= 27\%$ To change a fraction to a percentage,
  ii $\frac{9}{20}$ $= \frac{9}{20} \times 100\%$ $= 45\%$ multiply by 100

d Convert the following percentages to fractions.

  i 20%
  ii 85%

  i 20% $= \frac{20}{100} = \frac{20^{1}}{100_{5}}$ $= \frac{1}{5}$ To change a percentage to a fraction, put
  ii 85% $= \frac{85}{100} = \frac{85^{17}}{100_{20}}$ $= \frac{17}{20}$ it over 100 and cancel to lowest terms

To compare fractions, decimals and percentages, change them all to percentages

Apply 1

1 Change each decimal to a percentage.

   a 0.27   **c** 0.08   **e** 1.28   **g** 0.125

   b 0.15   **d** 0.8   **f** 3.4   **h** $0.\dot{3}$

2 Change each percentage to a decimal.

   a 44%   **e** 105%

   b 59%   **f** 225%

   c 70%   **g** 37.5%

   d 3%   **h** 14.25%

3 Change each fraction to a percentage.

   a $\frac{57}{100}$ **c** $\frac{3}{10}$ **e** $\frac{1}{5}$ **g** $\frac{13}{20}$

   b $\frac{7}{100}$ **d** $\frac{9}{50}$ **f** $\frac{12}{25}$ **h** $\frac{3}{8}$

4 Change each percentage to a fraction, in its simplest form.

   a 99%   **e** 8%

   b 30%   **f** 75%

   c 26%   **g** $7\frac{1}{2}$%

   d 55%   **h** 12.5%

5 Place these in order of size, smallest first.

   a $\frac{2}{5}$, 0.36, 42%   **b** 28%, $\frac{1}{4}$, 0.3   **c** 0.1, 9%, $\frac{2}{25}$

6 Jake says that 34% is less than a third.
   Is he right?

7 Gina says that one eighth is 1.25%.
   What mistake has she made?

8 Change each of these fractions to a percentage.

   $\frac{3}{5}$, $\frac{9}{20}$, $2\frac{2}{5}$, $\frac{8}{25}$

   Use your answers to fill in the number square, as if they are the answers
   to crossword clues. (One answer has been entered in the grid for you.)

Learn 2 Working out a percentage of a given quantity

Examples: **a** Find 35% of £5.40

Without a calculator	Using a calculator
10% = £5.40 ÷ 10 = 54p 5% = $\frac{1}{2}$ of 10% = 27p 10% 54p +10% +54p +10% +54p + 5% +27p 35% £1.89	1% = £5.40 ÷ 100 35% = £5.40 ÷ 100 × 35 = £1.89 or 35% = £0.35 0.35 × £5.40 = £1.89

b Calculate the simple interest on £300 for 2 years at 8%

Without a calculator	Using a calculator
8% of £100 = £8 8% of £300 = 3 × £8 = £24 For 2 years the interest is twice this : 2 × £24 = £48	8% = 8 ÷ 100 8 ÷ 100 × £300 = £24 For 2 years the interest is twice this : 2 × £24 = £48

$$\text{Formula: Simple interest} = \frac{\textbf{Principal} \times \textbf{Rate} \times \textbf{Time (in years)}}{100}$$

$$SI = \frac{P \times R \times T}{100}$$

Apply 2

Work out the following:

1 10% of 60 m

2 7% of £300

3 25% of £3.60

4 20% of 40 kg

5 80% of 40 kg

6 5% of £8.20

7 30% of 50 cm

8 15% of £70

9 75% of 9.6 m

10 $17\frac{1}{2}$% of £540

11 The simple interest on £400 for 2 years at 6% per annum

12 The simple interest on £200 for 7 years at 5% per annum

13 The simple interest on £1000 for 2 years at $4\frac{1}{2}$% per annum

14 The simple interest on £5000 for 3 years at 8% per annum

15 The final amount if £500 is invested for 4 years at simple interest of 3% per annum

Work out the following:

16 35% of £2.40

17 52% of £850

18 40% of 19.5 m

19 16% of £94.80

20 18% of 175 g

21 6% of £4.50

22 84% of 35 kg

23 27% of 60 cm

24 130% of £35.58

25 $37\frac{1}{2}$% of £11.52

26 The simple interest on £950 for 6 years at 7% per annum

27 The simple interest on £6520 for 4 years at 3.8% per annum

28 The simple interest on £4965 for 5 years at $12\frac{1}{2}$% per annum

29 The simple interest on £14 600 for 3 years at $5\frac{3}{4}$% per annum

30 The total owed if £1575 is borrowed for 2 years at simple interest of 14.2% per annum

Learn 3 Increasing or decreasing by a given percentage

Examples:

a Parveen's bus fare to town is 80p. The bus fares go up by 5%.
How much is the new fare?

10% of 80p = 8p 5% of 80p = 4p New fare = 84p	Original fare = 100% New fare = $(100 + 5)$% $= 105\% = 1.05$ New fare = 1.05×80p $= 84$p

b Find the new price of a £350 TV after a 4% reduction.

1% of £350 = £3.50 4% of £350 = £3.50 × 4 = £14 New price = £350 − £14 $= £336$	Original price = 100% New price = $(100 - 4)$% $= 96\% = 0.96$ New price = $0.96 \times £350$ $= £336$

Apply 3

1 Increase 25 cm by 10%.

2 Decrease 700 g by 5%.

3 Decrease £450 by 20%.

4 Increase £3 by 8%.

5 Get Real!
Todd is paid £300 per week.
He gets a 4% pay rise.
What is his new weekly pay?

6 Get Real!
A package holiday is priced at £660.
Gary gets a 10% discount for booking before the end of January.
How much does he pay?

7 Get Real!
Emma gets a 15% discount on purchases from Aqamart.
How much does she pay for a TV priced at £500?

8 Get Real!
Parveen's bus fare to town is 80p.
The bus fares go up by 5%.
How much will Parveen now have to pay to travel to town?

9 Increase 125 cm by 16%.

10 Increase 340 g by 5%.

11 Decrease £560 by 12%.

12 Decrease £9.50 by 22%.

13 Get Real!
The population of Baytown was 65 000 in 1990.
By the year 2000, Baytown's population had gone up by 27%.
What was the population in 2000?

14 Get Real!
Becky buys a new car for £12 000.
Over 2 years, it depreciates by 45%.
What is the value of the car after 2 years?

15 Get Real!
Liam sold 540 DVDs in June.
In July, his sales dropped by 15%.
How many DVDs did he sell in July?

16 Get Real!
The bill for a repair is £57.30
VAT at $17\frac{1}{2}$% has to be added to the bill.
What is the total cost of the repair?

Explore

◎ Kate wants to buy a music centre priced at £439

◎ She has to put down £100 deposit

◎ There are two ways she can pay the rest of the price (the balance)

  1 The EasyPay option:
- 10% credit charge on the balance
- 6 equal monthly payments.

  2 The PayLess option:
- 3% added each month to the amount owing at the beginning of the month
- pay £60 per month until the balance is paid off

(Note: in the last month Kate will only pay the remaining balance, not a full £60)

◎ Using a calculator, investigate these two options to advise Kate which one is best

◎ Would your advice be different if EasyPay charged 11% or PayLess charged $3\frac{1}{2}$% each month?

Investigate further

Learn 4 Expressing one quantity as a percentage of another

Examples:

a Express 27 g as a percentage of 300 g.

27 as a fraction of 300 is $\frac{27}{300}$

To convert a fraction to a percentage you multiply by 100:

$$\frac{{}^{9}\cancel{27}}{{}_{100}\cancel{300}} \times 100 = 9\%$$

Write them as a fraction and multiply by 100 to change to a percentage.

b Express 84p as a percentage of £20. *Make sure both quantities are in the **same units**.*

Working in pounds,
change 84p to £0.84

0.84 as a fraction of 20 is $\frac{0.84}{20}$

To convert a fraction to a
percentage you multiply by 100:

$$\frac{0.84}{20} = \frac{0.84}{20} \times 100\%$$

$$= \frac{0.84}{\cancel{20}_1} \times \cancel{100}^5 \%$$

$$= 4.2\%$$

Working in pence,
change £20 to 2000p

84 as a fraction of 2000 is $\frac{84}{2000}$

To convert a fraction to a
percentage you multiply by 100:

$$\frac{84}{2000} = \frac{84}{2000} \times 100\%$$

$$= \frac{\cancel{84}^{42}}{\cancel{2000}_{\cancel{1000}_{10}}} \times \cancel{100}^1 \%$$

$$= 4.2\%$$

Apply 4

1 Express £22 as a percentage of £200.

2 Express 12p as a percentage of 16p.

3 Express 20 kg as a percentage of 50 kg.

4 Express 21p as a percentage of £3.50.

5 Express 85 mm as a percentage of 10 cm.

6 Get Real!
There are 800 students in Uptown College.
96 of these students walk to college each day.
What percentage of the students walk to college?

7 Get Real!
Chris has 50 books on his shelves.
29 of these books are science fiction.
What percentage of his books are science fiction?

8 Get Real!
Kate has 6 girl cousins and 9 boy cousins.
What percentage of her cousins are boys?

 **9** Express £22.50 as a percentage of £450.

10 Express 7 cm as a percentage of 12.5 cm.

11 Express 65 g as a percentage of 5 kg.

12 Express £1190 as a percentage of £2800.

13 Express £17.64 as a percentage of £72.

14 Get Real!

Mel wanted to buy a sofa priced at £1450.
The salesman asked for a deposit of £348.
What percentage of the price was this?

15 Get Real!

Out of 3600 claims on household insurance,
522 were for broken windows.
What percentage of claims were for broken windows?

16 Get Real!

Grace has £6.25 in her purse.
She puts 20p in a charity box.
What percentage of her money has gone to charity?

Learn 5   Percentage increase and decrease

Examples:

a Find the percentage increase when the temperature goes up from 20 °C to 26 °C.

Temperature increase = 6°
6 as a fraction of 20 is $\frac{6}{20}$
To convert a fraction to a percentage you multiply by 100:

$$\frac{6}{20} = \frac{6}{20} \times 100\%$$

$$= \frac{6}{20_1} \times 100^5\%$$

$$= 30\% \text{ increase}$$

> Make sure both quantities are in the **same units**
>
> Write this as a fraction and multiply by 100 to change to a percentage (**The original quantity has to be on the bottom of the fraction**)

b Find the percentage decrease when the price of a toy falls from £12.50 to £11.75

Price decrease = £0.75
£0.75 as a fraction of £12.50 is $\frac{0.75}{12.50}$
To convert a fraction to a percentage you multiply by 100:

$$\frac{0.75}{12.50} = \frac{0.75}{12.50} \times 100\%$$

$$= \frac{0.75}{12.50_{25_1}} \times 100^{200^8}\%$$

$$= 6\% \text{ decrease}$$

c Find the percentage profit when an object is bought for £200 and sold for £256.

Price increase = £56

£56 as a fraction of £200 is $\frac{56}{200}$

To convert a fraction to a percentage you multiply by 100:

$$\frac{56}{200} = \frac{56}{200} \times 100\%$$

$$= \frac{56}{200_2} \times 100^1\%$$

$$= 28\% \text{ increase}$$

Apply 5

1 The price of a packet of biscuits goes up from 30p to 36p.
Find the percentage increase.

2 The price of a computer drops from £250 to £225.
Find the percentage decrease.

3 The population of a village goes up from 400 to 436.
Find the percentage increase.

4 Becky's curtains were 60 cm long before she washed them.
After the wash they were only 51 cm long.
Find the percentage decrease in length.

5 Sam buys a guitar for £125 and sells it for £160.
Find his percentage profit.

6 A landlord puts the rent on a flat up from £280 per month to £301 per month.
Find the percentage increase.

7 A music system was priced at £240.
In the sale, the price dropped to £186.
Find the percentage decrease.

8 The price of a house goes down from £166 000 to £141 100.
Find the percentage decrease.

9 Callum buys a car for £2450 and does some repairs.
He sells the car for £2989.
Find his percentage profit.

10 Zoe says the answer to question 9 is 18%.
What mistake has she made?

Percentages

The following exercise tests your understanding of this chapter, with the questions appearing in order of increasing difficulty.

1 Copy and complete the table below.
Write each fraction in its simplest form.

Decimal	Fraction	Percentage
0.3		
0.55		
0.875		
	$\frac{1}{3}$	
	$\frac{3}{4}$	
	$\frac{4}{5}$	
		1%
		$2\frac{1}{2}\%$
		48%
1.25		
	$2\frac{2}{3}$	
		320%

2 a Guy Fawkes bought a box of 75 matches to light his bonfire. The wood was damp and it took him 16% of his matches to light the fire. How many matches did he use?

b A DJ has 400 CDs, 65% of which are dance music.
How many dance music CDs does she have?

c A cricket team scored 256 runs altogether. Their leading batsman scored $37\frac{1}{2}\%$ of the runs. How many runs did he score?

d A shop assistant is paid 8% of all furniture sales as his monthly bonus. What bonus did he get on sales of £4600?

3 a Write 60p as a percentage of £1.20

b What is 150 m as a percentage of 3 km?

c David has bought Victoria an 18 carat gold bracelet.
Pure gold is 24 carat.
What percentage of Victoria's bracelet is gold?

d A bag of sand is labelled as 50 kg.
It actually contains 2.5% more.
How much sand does it contain?

e Ms Berry has picked 1.2 kg of blackberries for making jam.
She needs 15% more to make her recipe.
What weight of blackberries does the recipe require?

f The amount of evaporation while whisky is maturing in the vat is known in the trade as the 'Angel's Share'. A vat of whisky originally held 55 litres. Evaporation reduced this by 16%. How many litres were left in the vat after the angels had received their share?

4 a A book is designed to have 650 pages.
When the author finished the manuscript he found he had written 754 pages.
What percentage increase is this?

b A box of 144 pens is bought for £10 and the individual pens are sold at 10p each. What is the percentage profit?

c Toad of Toad Hall bought his latest car for £18 000. A week later he crashed it and, after repair, sold it for £11 700. What was his percentage loss?

d 100 apples are bought for £17 but 5% are found to be damaged and not saleable. The rest are sold at 20p each. What is the percentage profit?

e Pythagoras makes a calculator error while using his famous theorem! He wants to find the value of $\sqrt{112}$ but instead he finds $\sqrt{121}$. What is the percentage error in his calculation?

Try a real past exam question to test your knowledge:

5 a A year ago, Mark was 185 cm tall.
He is now 4.3% taller.
How tall is Mark now?

b A year ago Vicky weighed 151 lb.
She now weighs 164 lb.
Calculate the percentage increase in Vicky's weight.

Spec B, Module 3, Nov 02

7 Ratio and proportion

What you should already know ...

- How to add, subtract, multiply and divide numbers

- How to simplify fractions

VOCABULARY

Variable – a symbol representing a quantity that can take different values such as x, y or z

Constant – a number that does not change, for example, the formula $P = 4l$ states that the perimeter of a square is always four times the length of one side; 4 is a constant and P and l are variables

Ratio – the ratio of two or more numbers or quantities is a way of comparing their sizes, for example, if a school has 25 teachers and 500 students, the ratio of teachers to students is 25 to 500, or 25 : 500 (read as 25 to 500)

Unitary ratio – a ratio in the form $1 : n$ or $n : 1$; for example, for every 100 female babies born, 105 male babies are born. The ratio of the number of females to the number of males is 100 : 105; as a unitary ratio, this is 1 : 1.05, which means that, for every female born, 1.05 males are born

Proportion – if a class has 12 boys and 18 girls, the proportion of boys in the class is $\frac{12}{30}$, which simplifies to $\frac{2}{5}$, and the proportion of girls is $\frac{18}{30}$, which simplifies to $\frac{3}{5}$ (the **ratio** of boys to girls is 12 : 18, which simplifies to 2 : 3) – a proportion compares one part with the whole; a ratio compares parts with one another

Unitary method – a way of calculating quantities that are in proportion, for example, if 6 items cost £30 and you want to know the cost of 10 items, you can first find the cost of one item by dividing by 6, then find the cost of 10 by multiplying by 10

6 items cost £30

1 item costs $\dfrac{£30}{6} = £5$

10 items cost $10 \times £5 = £50$

75

Learn 1 Finding and simplifying ratios

Examples:

a A school has 50 teachers and 900 students.
Write down the teacher : student ratio and express it in its simplest form.

First write the numbers in the correct order for the ratio and separate them with a colon symbol.

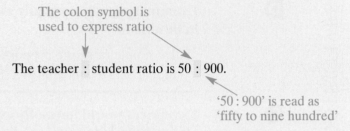

The colon symbol is used to express ratio

The teacher : student ratio is 50 : 900.

'50 : 900' is read as 'fifty to nine hundred'

Like cancelling a fraction, the ratio can be simplified.

Both numbers have been divided by 10

Ratio = 50 : 900 = 5 : 90 = 1 : 18

Both numbers have been divided by 5

$$\frac{50}{900} \xrightarrow{\div 10} = \frac{5}{90} \xrightarrow{\div 5} = \frac{1}{18}$$

This is like simplifying fractions

The ratio in its simplest form is 1 : 18.

This means that, for every teacher in this school, there are 18 students (or the number of teachers is $\frac{1}{18}$ of the number of students).

b A shopkeeper buys boxes of chocolates for £3.50 and sells them for £4.25
What is the ratio of the profit to the cost price?

The profit is the selling price minus the cost price = £4.25 − £3.50 = 75p.

Ratio of profit to cost price = 75p : £3.50

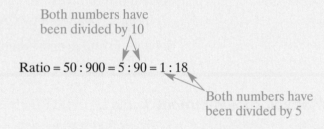

Make sure the amounts are both in pence or both in pounds. Using pence is probably easier

Divide both numbers by 5

= 75p : 350p

= 75 : 350

= 15 : 70

= 3 : 14

The ratio 75p to 350p is the same ratio as 75 to 350

Divide both numbers by 5 again, then the ratio cannot be simplified any more

$$\frac{75}{350} \xrightarrow{\div 5} = \frac{15}{70} \xrightarrow{\div 5} = \frac{3}{14}$$

Compare with the fraction simplification

The ratio of 3 to 14 means that the shopkeeper makes a profit of £3 for every £14 she spends on boxes of chocolates (if she sells them all).

It also means that:
- the profit is $\frac{3}{17}$ of the selling price
- the cost price is $\frac{14}{17}$ of the selling price.

Check that you can see where the numerators and denominators have come from.

Also check that $\frac{3}{17}$ of £4.25 is 75p and $\frac{14}{17}$ of £4.25 is £3.50

Apply 1

 1 Write each of these ratios as simply as possible.

a 2 : 4	**e** 2 : 12	**i** 24 : 36	**m** 0.3 : 0.8
b 2 : 6	**f** 2 : 14	**j** 25 : 100	**n** $2\frac{1}{2} : 7\frac{1}{2}$
c 2 : 8	**g** 12 : 36	**k** $\frac{2}{3} : \frac{4}{9}$	**o** 20% : 80%
d 2 : 10	**h** 18 : 24	**l** 1.5 : 2.5	**p** 25 : 200

 2 a Write down three different pairs of numbers that are in the ratio 1 : 2.

b Write down three different pairs of numbers that are in the ratio 1 : 4.

c Explain how to find pairs of numbers that are in the ratio 1 : 4.

d Pippa writes the three pairs of numbers 6 and 9, 9 and 12, and 12 and 15. She says these pairs of numbers are all in the same ratio. What has Pippa done wrong?

 3 Get Real!

A recipe for pastry needs 50 grams of butter and 100 grams of flour.

a What is the ratio of butter to flour? What is the ratio of flour to butter?

b How much butter is needed for 200 grams of flour?

c How much flour is needed for 30 grams of butter?

d What fraction is the butter's weight of the flour's weight?

4 Get Real!

On a music download site, a track costs 75p and an album costs £7.50

Find the ratio of the cost of a track to the cost of an album, A, in its simplest form.

5 Get Real!

A recipe for cheese sauce for four people needs these ingredients:

- 600 mℓ milk, warmed
- 100 g grated cheese
- 40 g flour
- 40 g butter
- seasoning

a List the ingredients needed to make enough cheese sauce for two people.

b Explain how to find how the quantities to make enough cheese sauce for ten people.

6 Get Real!

a Find, in their simplest forms, the teacher : student ratios for these schools.

School	Number of teachers	Number of students
School 1	75	1500
School 2	15	240
School 3	22	374
School 4	120	1800
School 5	65	1365

The numbers have been made simple so that it is easy for you to work them out. Real schools have harder numbers!

b i If a school with 50 teachers had the same teacher : student ratio as School 1, how many students would it have?

ii If a school with 2000 students had the same teacher : student ratio as School 1, how many teachers would it have?

c Which school has the 'best' teacher to student ratio? (That is, which school has the smallest number of students for each teacher?)

7 Get Real!

a Find the profit : cost price ratio for these items.

Item	Cost price	Selling price	Profit
Litre of petrol	85p		5p
Car	£4500	£5000	
Calculator	£15		£10
Book	£2.80	£3.50	
Magazine		£1.10	15p
Sandwich		£1.25	50p

b Use the profit : cost price ratio for the car to write fraction statements like those at the end of Learn **1**.

c In question **6**, all the ratios were in the form 1 : *something* (mathematically, 1 : n) so they were easy to compare.
How could you compare the ratios in part **a**? Would a calculator help?

8 **Get Real!**

a In a salsa class, the ratio of women to men is 5 : 4.

   i There are 10 women in the class. How many men are there?

   ii The number of women and the number of men both double. Does the ratio change? Explain your answer.

b In the jazz dance class, the ratio of men to women is 2 : 3 and there are 10 dancers altogether.

   i How many men and how many women are there in the jazz dance class?

   ii Two more men and two more women join the class. Does the ratio of men to women increase, decrease or stay the same? Explain your answer.

 9 The ratio $x : y$ simplifies to 3 : 4.

a If x is 6, what is y?   **c** If y is 2, what is x?

b If y is 12, what is x?   **d** If x and y add to 35, what are x and y?

10 Make up another question like question **9** and give the answers.

11 Here is a pattern sequence.

 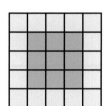 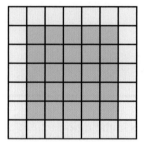

a Does the ratio 'number of green squares : number of yellow squares' increase, decrease or stay the same as the shapes get bigger? Show how you worked out your answer.

b Draw your own sequence where the ratio of the number of green squares to the number of yellow squares stays the same as the shapes get bigger.

Explore

Map scales are often expressed in ratio form, such as 1 : 100 000

- Look at some maps (perhaps you can use examples from geography)
- How are the scales of the maps shown? Write down some examples
- Find out what a scale in the form 1 : 100 000 means
- Find out how to express map scales such as '2 cm to 1 km' in ratio form
- What distance in real life does 3 cm on a 1 : 100 000 map represent?

Investigate further

Learn 2   Using ratios to find quantities

Example:

In a school of 1000 students, the ratio of boys to girls is 9 : 11. How many boys and how many girls are there in the school?

For this problem, you need to divide 1000 students in the ratio 9 : 11 to find the number of boys and the number of girls.

The ratio shows that *for every* 9 boys there are 11 girls. So *in every* 20 students, there are 9 boys and 11 girls, as 9 + 11 = 20.

Out of every 20 students, 9 are boys

Out of every 20 students, 11 are girls

The fraction of boys in the school is $\frac{9}{20}$ and the fraction of girls is $\frac{11}{20}$

The number of boys in the school is $\frac{9}{20}$ of 1000.

$$\frac{1}{20} \text{ of } 1000 = \frac{1000}{20} = 50$$

So $\frac{9}{20}$ of $1000 = 50 \times 9 = 450$

The number of girls in the school is $\frac{11}{20}$ of 1000, which is $11 \times 50 = 550$.

So the number of boys is 450 and the number of girls is 550.

Check that the number of boys and the number of girls add up to 1000, the total number of students in the school

Apply 2

 1 Divide these numbers and quantities in the ratio 1 : 2.

    a 150   **c** £4.50   **e** £1.50

    b 300   **d** 6 litres   **f** 1.5 litres

 **2** Divide the numbers and quantities in question **1** in the ratio 2 : 3.

 **3** Divide the numbers and quantities in question **1** in the ratio 3 : 7.

4 Divide the numbers and quantities in question **1** in the ratio 1 : 3 : 6.

5 Get Real!

Pastry is made from fat and flour in the ratio 1 : 2.

    a How much flour is needed to make 150 g of pastry?

    b How much fat is needed to make 6 ounces of pastry?

    c How much pastry can you make if you have plenty of flour but only 60 g of fat?

6 *You should be able to do the first four of these schools without a calculator but you will need one for School E and for parts **b** and **c**.*

   a Find the number of boys and the number of girls in these schools.

School	Total number of students	Boy:girl ratio
School A	750	1:1
School B	900	4:5
School C	1800	4:5
School D	1326	6:7
School E	1184	301:291

School E shows the most realistic ratio. What is the boy : girl ratio in your school or college?

   b Find the boy : girl ratios in part **a** in the form 1 : *n* (in other words, find how many girls there are for every boy).

   c Which school has the largest proportion of boys? Give a reason for your answer.

7 This table shows the ratio of carbohydrate to fat to protein in some foods.

   a Find the amount of fat in 150 g of each of the foods.

Food	Carbohydrate : fat : protein
Chicken sandwich	1 : 1 : 1
Grilled salmon	0 : 1 : 1
Yoghurt (whole milk)	1 : 2 : 1
Taco chips	10 : 4 : 1
Bread	7 : 2 : 1
Milk	2 : 3 : 2

> **HINT** Use a calculator for milk as the ratios do not work out easily. Round your answers to the nearest 5 grams.

   b Which of these foods would you avoid if you were on a low-fat diet?

   c How many grams of yoghurt would you need to eat to have 100 g of protein?

   d Which of these foods would you avoid if you were on a low-carbohydrate diet?

8 Two people, Jamil and Jane, invested money in a business. Jamil invested £3450 and Jane invested £5500. At the end of the financial year, the profit is split between Jamil and Jane in the ratio of their investments. The profit is £7350. How much do Jamil and Jane each receive?

9 Bronze for coins can be made of copper, tin and zinc in the ratio 95 : 4 : 1.

   a How much of each metal is needed to make 1 kilogram of bronze?

   b How much of each metal is needed to make 10 kilograms of bronze?

   c How much of each metal is needed to make half a kilogram of bronze?

   d How much zinc would there be in a coin weighing 6 grams?

Learn 3   Ratio and proportion

Example:

A teacher pays £27.60 for 6 calculators.
How much does he pay for 15 of the same calculators?

A useful method for finding quantities in proportion, or to solve 'best buy' problems, is the unitary method (shown below).

Write the statement with the number you want to change (the number of calculators) at the start

6 calculators cost £27.60

Next write the statement starting with 1

When you know the cost of 1 calculator you can find the cost of any number

1 calculator costs $\dfrac{£27.60}{6} = £4.60$

Divide the cost of 6 calculators by 6 to find the cost of 1 calculator

15 calculators cost $15 \times £4.60 = £69$

Finally, write the statement starting with the number you want (15 in this case)

Multiply the cost of 1 calculator by 15 to find the cost of 15 calculators

Check that the answer is reasonable
Do an estimate: the cost of 15 calculators is between 2 and 3 times the cost of 6 calculators

All the calculating can be left to the end if you prefer:

6 calculators cost £27.60

1 calculator costs $\dfrac{£27.60}{6}$

15 calculators cost $15 \times \dfrac{£27.60}{6} = £69$

This is the same as
$\dfrac{£27.60}{6} \times 1.5$ or $£27.60 \times \dfrac{15}{6}$

If you feel confident with problems like this, you can do them in one step by combining the multiplication and division, but be careful and check that your answer is sensible

Apply 3

1 Get Real!

Check that, in the example above, the ratio 'cost of 1 calculator : cost of 6 calculators : cost of 15 calculators' is 1 : 6 : 15.

 2 Get Real!

Sajid worked for 8 hours and was paid £30.

a How much will he be paid for working 10 hours at the same rate of pay?

b Complete a copy of this table. Plot the values in the table as points on a graph, using the numbers of hours worked as the *x*-coordinates and the money earned as the corresponding *y*-coordinates.

Number of hours worked	0	2	4	6	8	10
Money earned (£)					30	

c The points should lie in a straight line through (0, 0).

  i Explain why.

  ii Show how to use the graph to find out how much Sajid earns in 5 hours.

3 Get Real!

50 grams of fish food will feed 8 fish for 1 day.

a How much food would 12 fish require for 1 day?

b How many days can 2 fish survive on 50 grams of food?

c How much food is needed for 10 fish for 7 days?

4 Get Real!

Lovelylocks shampoo is sold in travel size and large size.

	Amount of shampoo	Price
Travel size	40 grams	75p
Large size	125 grams	£2.25

Calculate which of the two sizes gives you better value for money.
Show all your working clearly.

5 Get Real!

'Rich and Dark' chocolate is sold in a 55 g size costing 60p and a 100 g size costing £1.05. Which of these is better value for money?

6 Get Real!

On the motorway, Jacob drove a distance of 84 miles in 3 hours.

a How far would Jacob travel in 4 hours at the same average speed?

b How far would he go in three-quarters of an hour at this average speed?

c How long would it take for Jacob to travel 60 miles at this average speed?

7 Get Real!

Notice that the two parts of this question are really the same!
Use part **a** to help you work out part **b**.

a 80% of a number is 16. Use the unitary method to find 100% of the number.

b A sweater is reduced by 20% to £16 in the sale.
What was the original price of the sweater?

8 a Two numbers are in the ratio 1 : 0.75
   The first number is 12; what is the second?

   b Two numbers are in the ratio 1 : 0.75
   The second number is 12; what is the first?

   c Three numbers are in the ratio 1.1 : 1 : 0.9
   The third number is 36; what are the other two numbers?

9 Get Real!

The weights of objects on other planets are proportional to their weights on Earth. A person weighing 120 pounds on Earth would weigh 20 pounds on the moon and 300 pounds on Jupiter.

a What would a teenager weighing 80 pounds on Earth weigh on Jupiter?

b What would a rock weighing 10 kilograms on the moon weigh on Earth?

c This graph shows the weights of objects on Jupiter compared with their weights on Earth.

Copy the graph and sketch a line on it to show the weights of objects on the moon compared with their weights on Earth.

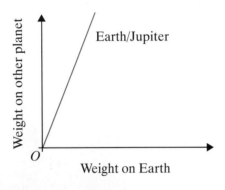

d Express the ratio 'weight of object on Earth : weight of object on moon : weight of object on Jupiter' in its simplest form.

Explore

You may already know something about the Fibonacci sequences

Each term is found by adding together the last two terms

So, starting with 1, 1, the series continues 1, 1, 2, 3, 5, 8, ...

◎ Carry the sequence on until you have at least 20 terms (would a spreadsheet be useful?)

◎ Work out, in the form $1 : n$, the ratio of
  term 1 to term 2
  term 2 to term 3
  term 3 to term 4 and so on

◎ What can you say about the ratios as you go through the series?

Investigate further

Ratio and proportion

The following exercise tests your understanding of this chapter,
with the questions appearing in order of increasing difficulty.

 1 a Write each of the following ratios in its simplest form:

    i $6:8$

    ii $27:81$

    iii $1000:10$

    iv $\frac{1}{4}:2$

    v $3\frac{1}{2}:2\frac{1}{3}$

  b i In a choir there are 12 boys and 18 girls.
     Express this as a ratio in its simplest form.

    ii Two more boys and two more girls join the choir.
     Express the new ratio in its simplest form.

2 a 2400 people voted in a local election.
    Votes for the three candidates were in the ratio $5:6:9$.
    How many votes did each candidate get?

  b A drink is made up of water, orange and lemon in the ratio $5:1:2$.
    Find the amount of water, orange and lemon in a 1 litre bottle.

3 a In a gym the ratio of women members to men members is $5:4$.
    There are 85 women members.
    How many men members are there?

  b Jamie is cooking omelettes.
    To make omelettes for 4 people he uses 6 eggs.
    How many eggs does Jamie need to make omelettes for 10 people?

c The supermarkets 'Lessprice' and 'Lowerpay' both sell packs of pens.
'Lessprice' sells a pack of 5 pens for £1.25
'Lowerpay' sells a pack of 6 pens for £1.44
Which supermarket gives the greater value?

d Two circles have radii of 5 cm and 6 cm respectively.
What is the ratio of:

  i their circumferences

  ii their areas?

e It takes Kelly 25 seconds to run 200 m.
At the same pace, how long will it take her to run:

  i 56 m

  ii 128 m?

Try a real past exam question to test your knowledge:

4 The sizes of the interior angles of a quadrilateral are in the ratio
3 : 4 : 6 : 7.
Calculate the size of the largest angle.

Spec B, Int Paper 2, Nov 03

Glossary

Amount – the total you will have in the bank or the total you will owe the bank, at the end of the period of time

Balance – the amount of money you have in your bank account or the amount of money you owe after you have paid a deposit

Common factor – factors that are in common for two or more numbers, for example,

the factors of 6 are 1, 2, 3, 6
the factors of 9 are 1, 3, 9
the common factors are 1 and 3

Common fraction – see fraction

Constant – a number that does not change, for example, the formula $P = 4l$ states that the perimeter of a square is always four times the length of one side; 4 is a constant and P and l are variables

Counting number or **natural number** – a positive whole number, for example, 1, 2, 3, ...

Credit – when you buy goods 'on credit' you do not pay all the cost at once; instead you make a number of payments at regular intervals, often once a month

Cube number – a cube number is the outcome when a number is multiplied by itself then multiplied by itself again

Cube root – the cube root of a number such as 125 is a number whose outcome is 125 when multiplied by itself then multiplied by itself again

Decimal – a number in which a decimal point separates the whole number part from the decimal part, for example, 24.8

Decimal fraction – a fraction consisting of tenths, hundredths, thousandths, and so on, expressed in a decimal form, for example, 0.65 (6 tenths and 5 hundredths)

Decimal places – the digits to the right of a decimal point in a number, for example, in the number 23.657, the number 6 is the first decimal place (worth $\frac{6}{10}$), the number 5 is the second decimal place (worth $\frac{5}{100}$) and 7 is the third decimal place (worth $\frac{7}{1000}$); the number 23.657 has 3 decimal places

Denominator – the number on the bottom of a fraction

Deposit – an amount of money you pay towards the cost of an item, with the rest of the cost to be paid later

Depreciation – a reduction in value, for example, due to age or condition

Digit – any of the numerals from 0 to 9

Directed number – a number with a positive or negative sign attached to it; it is often seen as a temperature, for example, $-1, +1, +5, -3°C, +2°C, ...$

Discount – a reduction in the price, perhaps for paying in cash or paying early

Equivalent fraction – a fraction that has the same value as another, for example,
$\frac{3}{5}$ is equivalent to $\frac{30}{50}, \frac{6}{10}, \frac{60}{100}, \frac{15}{25}, \frac{1.5}{2.5}, ...$

Estimate – find an approximate value of a calculation; this is usually found by rounding all of the numbers to one significant figure, for example,
$\frac{20.4 \times 4.3}{5.2}$ is approximately $\frac{20 \times 4}{5}$ where each number is rounded to 1 s.f., the answer can be worked out in your head to give 16

Exponent – see index

Factor – a natural number which divides exactly into another number (no remainder); for example, the factors of 12 are 1, 2, 3, 4, 6, 12

Fraction or **simple fraction** or **common fraction** or **vulgar fraction** – a number written as one whole number over another, for example, $\frac{3}{8}$ (three eighths), which has the same value as $3 \div 8$

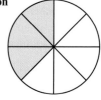

Greater than (>) – the number on the left-hand side of the sign is larger than that on the right-hand side

Highest common factor (HCF) – the highest factor that two or more numbers have in common, for example,

the factors of 16 are 1, 2, 4, 8, 16
the factors of 24 are 1, 2, 3, 4, 6, 8, 12, 24
the common factors are 1, 2, 4, 8
the highest common factor is 8

Improper fraction or **top-heavy fraction** – a fraction in which the numerator is bigger than the denominator, for example, $\frac{13}{5}$, which is equal to the mixed number $2\frac{3}{5}$

Index or **power** or **exponent** – the index tells you how many times the base number is to be multiplied by itself

So $5^3 = 5 \times 5 \times 5$

Index notation – when a product such as $2 \times 2 \times 2 \times 2$ is written as 2^4, the number 4 is the index (plural **indices**)

Indices – the plural of index

Integer – any positive or negative whole number or zero, for example, $-2, -1, 0, 1, 2, \ldots$

Interest – money paid to you by a bank, building society or other financial institution if you put your money in an account or the money you pay for borrowing from a bank

Least common multiple (LCM) – the least multiple which is common to two or more numbers, for example,

the multiples of 3 are 3, 6, 9, 12, 15, 18, 24, 27, 30, 33, 36, ...
the multiples of 4 are 4, 8, 12, 16, 20, 24, 28, 32, 36, ...
the common multiples are 12, 24, 36, ...
the least common multiple is 12

Less than ($<$) – the number on the left-hand side of the sign is smaller than that on the right-hand side

Lower bound – this is the minimum possible value of a measurement, for example, if a length is measured as 37 cm correct to the nearest centimetre, the lower bound of the length is 36.5 cm

Mixed number or **mixed fraction** – a number made up of a whole number and a fraction, for example, $2\frac{3}{5}$, which is equal to the improper fraction $\frac{13}{5}$

Multiple – the multiples of a number are the products of the multiplication tables, for example, the multiples of 3 are 3, 6, 9, 12, 15, ...

Natural number – see counting number

Negative number – a number less than 0; it is written with a negative sign, for example, $-1, -3, -7, -11, \ldots$

Numerator – the number on the top of a fraction

Numerator⟶ $\frac{3}{8}$ ⟵Denominator

Percentage – a number of parts per hundred, for example, 15% means $\frac{15}{100}$

Positive number – a number greater than 0; it can be written with or without a positive sign, for example, 1, $+4, 8, 9, +10, \ldots$

Power – see index

Prime number – a natural number with exactly two factors, for example, 2 (factors are 1 and 2), 3 (factors are 1 and 3), 5 (factors are 1 and 5), 7, 11, 13, 17, 23, ..., 59, ...

Principal – the money put into the bank or borrowed from the bank

Product – the result of multiplying together two (or more) numbers, variables, terms or expressions

Proper fraction – a fraction in which the numerator is smaller than the denominator, for example, $\frac{5}{13}$

Proportion – if a class has 12 boys and 18 girls, the proportion of boys in the class is $\frac{12}{30}$, which simplifies to $\frac{2}{5}$, and the proportion of girls is $\frac{18}{30}$, which simplifies to $\frac{3}{5}$ (the **ratio** of boys to girls is 12 : 18, which simplifies to 2 : 3) – a proportion compares one part with the whole; a ratio compares parts with one another

Rate – the percentage at which interest is added, usually expressed as per cent per annum (year)

Ratio – the ratio of two or more numbers or quantities is a way of comparing their sizes, for example, if a school has 25 teachers and 500 students, the ratio of teachers to students is 25 to 500, or 25 : 500 (read as 25 to 500)

Reciprocal – any number multiplied by its reciprocal equals one; one divided by a number will give its reciprocal, for example,
the reciprocal of 3 is $\frac{1}{3}$ because $3 \times \frac{1}{3} = 1$

Recurring decimal – a decimal with a repeating digit or group of digits, for example, 0.33333333333 ... (written as $0.\dot{3}$) or 0.25678678678678 ... (written as $0.25\dot{6}7\dot{8}$)

Round – give an approximate value of a number; numbers can be rounded to the nearest 1000, nearest 100, nearest 10, nearest integer, significant figures, decimal places, ... etc.

Significant figures – the digits in a number; the closer a digit is to the beginning of a number then the more important or significant it is; for example, in the number 23.657, 2 is the most significant digit and is worth 20, 7 is the least significant digit and is worth $\frac{7}{1000}$; the number 23.657 has 5 significant digits

Simplify a fraction or **express a fraction in its simplest form** – to change a fraction to the simplest equivalent fraction; to do this divide the numerator and the denominator by a common factor (this process is called cancelling or reducing or simplifying the fraction)

Simple fraction – see fraction

Square number – a square number is the outcome when a number is multiplied by itself

Square root – a square root of a number such as 16 is a number whose outcome is 16 when multiplied by itself

Sum – to find the sum of two numbers, you add them together

Terminating decimal – a decimal that ends, for example, 0.3, 0.33 or 0.3333

Time – usually measured in years for the purpose of working out interest

Top-heavy fraction – see improper fraction

Unitary method – a way of calculating quantities that are in proportion, for example, if 6 items cost £30 and you want to know the cost of 10 items, you can first find the cost of one item by dividing by 6, then find the cost of 10 by multiplying by 10

6 items cost £30

1 item costs $\dfrac{£30}{6}$ = £5

10 items cost 10 × £5 = £50

Unitary ratio – a ratio in the form $1 : n$ or $n : 1$; for example, for every 100 female babies born, 105 male babies are born. The ratio of the number of females to the number of males is 100 : 105; as a unitary ratio, this is 1 : 1.05, which means that, for every female born, 1.05 males are born

Unit fraction – a fraction with a numerator of 1, for example, $\frac{1}{5}$

Upper bound – this is the maximum possible value of a measurement, for example, if a length is measured as 37 cm correct to the nearest centimetre, the upper bound of the length is 37.5 cm

Variable – a symbol representing a quantity that can take different values such as x, y or z

VAT (Value Added Tax) – a tax that has to be added on to the price of goods or services

Vulgar fraction – see fraction